"*The Future of Blockchain in Tourism and Hospitality: Global Insights* offers a contribution in terms of additional exploration and reflection of the outcomes of previous studies on blockchain technology in the tourism sector. According to the outcomes of the chapters, blockchain cannot be considered yet as a valid solution for the problems afflicting tourism. More research is needed and more investigations on the advantages and disadvantages of real applications is required before being able to express a rational and motivated judgement on the question. For this reason, this new book is welcome, therefore and a useful contribution to the debate. Dr Fatima Zahra Fakir and Dr Erdem Baydeniz are to be commended on this extension to the debate."

Professor Marco Valeri, *Associate Professor, Niccolò Cusano University, Italy*

"This book offers readers an in-depth examination of the growing impact of blockchain technology in the hospitality and tourism sectors. As blockchain becomes increasingly prevalent worldwide, it enhances the security of big data records, improves transparency and trust among stakeholders, and facilitates smart contracts and decentralized loyalty programs. This technology also contributes to reducing costs and streamlining operations. The efficiency and potential of blockchain are reshaping the future of hospitality and tourism on a global scale."

Professor Ahmad Albattat, *Associate Professor, Management and Science University, Malaysia*

"*The Future of Blockchain in Tourism and Hospitality: Global Insights* is an innovative book that explores the revolutionary possibilities of blockchain technology in the tourism and hospitality industries. This comprehensive publication consolidates professional perspectives from many regions, providing readers with a profound comprehension of how blockchain technology may fundamentally transform businesses, improve consumer experiences, and guarantee heightened levels of security and transparency. This book is a must-read for professionals in the industry, academics, and technology aficionados. It provides valuable insights and guidance for developing creative applications and making strategic advancements in a fast-changing environment."

Dr. Viana Hassan, *Associate Professor, University of Malta, Malta*

The Future of Blockchain in Tourism and Hospitality

This timely and innovative book presents a critical exploration of how blockchain technologies may be useful in enhancing the sustainability, viability, and social responsibility of the tourism and hospitality sectors.

A key component of many contemporary financial structures and exchanges globally, this volume explores the international scope and application of blockchain within the tourism and hospitality industries, including varied and illustrative case studies from the vibrant streets of Tokyo to the serene landscapes of New Zealand. This book traverses diverse destinations to showcase the transformative power of blockchain in shaping travel experience, including insights into booking platforms, payment systems, loyalty programs, smart contracts, automation, and security issues. Strategic guidance for leveraging blockchain to address industry-specific challenges, maximize emerging opportunities, and promote transparency, trust, and sustainability is provided throughout.

This volume is a pivotal resource for students, scholars, and academics with an interest in digital innovation and analytics, new technologies in tourism and management, big data management and contemporary issues in marketing and management. The book may also be of professional interest to tourism and hospitality managers, marketers, consultants, and advisors.

Fatima Zahra Fakir obtained a Ph.D. in Economics and Sustainable Tourism and is currently an Assistant Professor and Researcher at the Department of Economics and Business Sciences, University of

Padova (DSEA). Her research interests include smart tourism, sustainable development, and cultural heritage.

Erdem Baydeniz is currently a lecturer at Aydın Adnan Menderes University. He has authored several national and international articles, papers, and book chapters, and his research interests include gastronomy, neurogastroenterology, and the dynamics of tourism management, such as sustainability, crisis management, and the resilience of tourism destinations.

Routledge Focus on Tourism and Hospitality

Routledge Focus on Tourism and Hospitality presents small books on big topics and how they intersect with the world of tourism and hospitality research. The idea is to fill the gap between journal article and book. This new short form series offers both established and early-career academics the flexibility to publish cutting-edge commentary on key areas of tourism and hospitality, topical issues, policy-focused research, analytical or theoretical innovations, a summary of the key players or short topics for specialized audiences in a succinct way.

Managing People in Commercial Kitchens
A Contemporary Approach
Charalampos Giousmpasoglou, Evangelia Marinakou, Anastasios Zopiatis and John Cooper

Smart Tourism Destination Governance
Technology and Design-Based Approach
Tomáš Gajdošík

Solo Travel, Tourism and Loneliness
A Critical Sociology
Hugues Séraphin and Maximiliano E. Korstanje

The Future of Blockchain in Tourism and Hospitality
Global Insights
Fatima Zahra Fakir and Erdem Baydeniz

For more information about this series, please visit: www.routledge.com/tourism/series/FTH

The Future of Blockchain in Tourism and Hospitality
Global Insights

Fatima Zahra Fakir and Erdem Baydeniz

LONDON AND NEW YORK

First published 2025
by Routledge
4 Park Square, Milton Park, Abingdon, Oxon OX14 4RN

and by Routledge
605 Third Avenue, New York, NY 10158

Routledge is an imprint of the Taylor & Francis Group, an informa business

© 2025 Fatima Zahra Fakir and Erdem Baydeniz

The right of Fatima Zahra Fakir and Erdem Baydeniz to be identified as authors of
this work has been asserted in accordance with sections 77 and 78 of the Copyright,
Designs and Patents Act 1988.

All rights reserved. No part of this book may be reprinted or reproduced or utilised
in any form or by any electronic, mechanical, or other means, now known or
hereafter invented, including photocopying and recording, or in any information
storage or retrieval system, without permission in writing from the publishers.

Trademark notice: Product or corporate names may be trademarks or registered
trademarks, and are used only for identification and explanation without intent to
infringe.

British Library Cataloguing-in-Publication Data
A catalogue record for this book is available from the British Library

ISBN: 978-1-032-86156-2 (hbk)
ISBN: 978-1-032-86164-7 (pbk)
ISBN: 978-1-003-52161-7 (ebk)

DOI: 10.4324/9781003521617

Typeset in Times New Roman
by Newgen Publishing UK

Contents

List of illustrations xi

Introduction 1

1 Blockchain in tourism and hospitality 5

2 Blockchain in tourism: Opportunities and applications 34

3 Smart contracts and automation in the travel industry 51

4 Blockchain's role in promoting sustainable tourism
practices 65

5 Future trends and challenges 83

6 Regulatory environment and ethical considerations 120

7 Strategies to encourage user adoption of blockchain
technology 129

8 Blockchain's potential impacts on justice, transparency,
and social equity 136

x *Contents*

Conclusion   146

References   *149*
Index   *170*

Illustrations

Figures

1.1	Transaction flow in blockchain technology	28
1.2	Calculation of Merkle root hash	30
1.3	Different components of the blockchain technology stack	33
3.1	Blockchain applications	52
5.1	Key blockchain applications for advancing tourism	84

Tables

5.1	Emerging trends in blockchain and tourism	98
5.2	BCT challenges	112

Introduction

In the contemporary landscape where technological advancements are rapidly revolutionizing various sectors, the travel industry is undergoing a significant transformation propelled by the adoption of advanced travel technologies. These innovations are not only enhancing consumer experiences in planning, booking, and executing travel but are also optimizing operational efficiencies for service providers. The incorporation of sophisticated IT solutions in airline and hospitality services is facilitating more efficient, personalized, and seamless travel experiences. This digital transformation is catalyzing substantial growth in the global travel technologies market.

According to a 2023 report by Research and Markets, 'the travel technologies market,' which was valued at US$5.4 billion in 2022, is projected to nearly double to US$10.7 billion by 2030. This expansion represents a compound annual growth rate (CAGR) of 8.8% from 2022 to 2030. A particularly robust segment within this market is the Airline and Hospitality IT Solutions sector, expected to grow at an impressive 11% CAGR over the next eight years.

Geographically, the United States remains a key player, with its market estimated at US$1.4 billion in 2022. Meanwhile, China is anticipated to exhibit significant growth, with a market size projected to reach US$2.6 billion by 2030, underpinned by a 10.2% CAGR. Other regions, including Japan, Canada, and Europe, are also set to contribute to this upward trajectory, each demonstrating positive growth prospects. The dynamic expansion of the travel technologies market highlights the increasing reliance on technological advancements to enhance travel experiences and operational efficiencies across the globe.

DOI: 10.4324/9781003521617-1

2 Introduction

Therefore, the tourism and travel industry continues to witness substantial investments aimed at harnessing technology to elevate the visitor experience, driven by the lucrative revenue streams generated through international tourism annually (Halkiopoulos, Antonopoulou, and Kostopoulos, 2023). This expansion trajectory reflects the dynamic nature of the industry, driven by various factors including technological advancements, evolving consumer preferences, and the increasing integration of digital solutions within the travel sector. Hence, travelers are increasingly reliant on a plethora of applications both pre- and during their trips, underscoring the pivotal role of technology in shaping their overall tourism experience.

Blockchain technology, initially synonymous with financial transactions, has emerged as a transformative tool with applications extending beyond its original scope. Within the realm of smart tourism, blockchain serves as a reliable and efficient platform connecting travelers with tourism products, addressing critical issues related to trust, security, and transparency (Treiblmaier, 2021). For instance, blockchain can streamline booking processes, verify traveler identities, and securely manage loyalty programs, thereby enhancing the overall travel experience. However, while the potential of blockchain for enhancing operational efficiency and secure transactions is widely recognized, its broader implications for the entire tourism value chain remain relatively underexplored (Thees, Erschbamer, and Pechlaner, 2020). Existing research highlights the technology's capability to revolutionize aspects such as payment processing, supply chain management, and data interoperability within the industry. Yet, comprehensive studies on its integration and long-term impact on the tourism sector are sparse. Thus, this study seeks to bridge this gap by addressing the following research question: How can blockchain technology be effectively integrated into the tourism and hospitality industry to enhance operational efficiency, trust, and security while overcoming existing regulatory and standardization challenges? Through a multidisciplinary approach, this research aims to provide a detailed analysis of blockchain's potential to transform the tourism landscape, offering insights into practical implementation strategies and policy recommendations.

To comprehensively explore this question, an exploratory methodology will be adopted, focusing on a multifaceted approach

Introduction 3

incorporating detailed literature reviews and in-depth case studies. The literature review component will delve into existing academic papers, industry reports, and case studies to identify prevailing trends, challenges, and potential solutions concerning blockchain technology in tourism and hospitality.

By synthesizing insights from a diverse array of sources, this review aims to provide a robust foundational understanding of the current state of research and practical applications in the field. Additionally, this study will conduct detailed case studies on successful blockchain implementations within the tourism industry and related sectors. These case studies will encompass a broad spectrum of applications, ranging from secure booking systems and loyalty programs to data security protocols. By examining real-world examples of blockchain integration, this research endeavors to extract valuable insights into the opportunities and challenges associated with leveraging blockchain technology in the tourism and hospitality domain.

Thus, this book delves into various facets of blockchain technology's impact on the tourism and hospitality industry. It begins with an "Introduction" elucidating the fundamentals of blockchain, its key features, and its applications across different sectors. The subsequent chapter, "Blockchain in tourism: Opportunities and applications," navigates through the challenges confronting the tourism sector, exploring how blockchain can address issues of security, trust, and sustainability. A focus on "Smart contracts and automation in the travel Industry" follows, providing technical insights and regulatory considerations alongside security challenges. The narrative then shifts toward "Blockchain's role in promoting sustainable tourism practices," investigating its role in promoting sustainable practices and integrating with responsible tourism initiatives. "Future trends and challenges" probes emerging trends in blockchain and tourism while addressing hurdles to widespread adoption and offering recommendations for stakeholders and policymakers. The discussion extends to the "Regulatory environment and ethical considerations," examining the regulatory framework, data privacy concerns, and ethical implications. "Strategies to encourage user adoption of blockchain technology" explores methods to engage tourism communities, enhance user training, and improve the overall user experience. Lastly, "Blockchain's potential impacts on justice, transparency, and

4 Introduction

social equity" highlights case studies, failures, and successes, offering insights and best practices from successful implementations. Through these chapters, the book comprehensively explores the transformative potential of blockchain technology in the tourism and hospitality domain.

1 Blockchain in tourism and hospitality

The tourism and hospitality sectors are experiencing rapid digital transformation, driven by emerging technologies that promise to revolutionize traditional operations. Among these technologies, blockchain stands out due to its potential to enhance transparency, security, and efficiency in various processes. As a digital ledger that records secure transactions across a decentralized network, blockchain technology offers significant advantages over traditional centralized systems. Its use of cryptographic hashing and consensus algorithms ensures that data is immutable and transparent, fostering trust and reducing the risk of fraud and data tampering (Awerika et al., 2023.

Blockchain's decentralized nature means that no single entity has control over the entire data set, which is maintained by a network of nodes, each holding a complete copy of the blockchain. This feature is particularly relevant in industries like tourism and hospitality, where multiple stakeholders, including travel agencies, hotels, and service providers, need to collaborate seamlessly. Blockchain's inherent transparency allows all participants in the network to view recorded transactions, promoting an environment of trust and accountability (Edastama et al., 2021; Lutfiani et al., 2022).

Security is another critical attribute of blockchain technology. Transactions are encrypted, and each is linked to the previous one through a unique hash, making unauthorized changes detectable and ensuring data integrity (Any et al., 2024). The consensus mechanisms, such as proof of work (PoW) and proof of stake (PoS), further enhance blockchain's reliability by requiring agreement among distributed nodes to validate transactions. These mechanisms prevent any single entity from altering the blockchain without consensus,

DOI: 10.4324/9781003521617-2

maintaining the integrity and consistency of the data (Huseynov and Mitchell, 2024).

As blockchain technology continues to evolve, its applications extend beyond cryptocurrencies into various sectors, including tourism and hospitality. This study explores the future of blockchain in these industries, highlighting its potential to transform operations, enhance customer experiences, and streamline processes. We will examine how blockchain can be leveraged to address challenges in booking systems, payment processing, identity verification, supply chain management, and customer loyalty programs.

Fundamentals of blockchain

Blockchain technology, at its core, is a distributed ledger that maintains a record of transactions across a network of computers (nodes) in a secure, transparent, and immutable manner. Each transaction is recorded in a block, and these blocks are linked in a chronological chain, creating an unalterable history of transactions (Awerika et al., 2023).

The process begins when a transaction is initiated, which is then broadcast to a peer-to-peer (P2P) network of computers known as nodes. These nodes validate the transaction using predefined consensus algorithms, such as PoW or PoS. Once validated, the transaction is grouped with other transactions to form a block, which is then added to the blockchain in a linear, chronological order (Edastama et al., 2021).

Each block contains a unique cryptographic hash of the previous block, a timestamp, and transaction data. This hash functions like a digital fingerprint, ensuring the integrity of the data within the block. If any data in the block is altered, the hash changes, breaking the chain and signaling a potential breach (Any et al., 2024).

Security and transparency

Blockchain's security and transparency are two of its most significant advantages. The decentralized nature of the blockchain means that no single entity controls the data, reducing the risk of centralized data breaches. Instead, the data is distributed across a network of nodes, each holding a copy of the entire blockchain (Huseynov and Mitchell, 2024). The transparency of blockchain

Blockchain in tourism and hospitality 7

comes from its public ledger, where all transactions are visible to network participants. This visibility fosters trust and accountability among users, as every transaction can be traced back to its origin (Lutfiani et al., 2022).

Consensus mechanisms

Consensus mechanisms are protocols used to achieve agreement on the state of the blockchain among distributed nodes. They play a crucial role in maintaining the integrity and security of the blockchain. The two most common consensus mechanisms are PoW and PoS.

PoW: PoW requires nodes, known as miners, to solve complex mathematical puzzles to validate transactions and create new blocks. This process is computationally intensive and consumes significant energy. The first miner to solve the puzzle gets to add the block to the blockchain and is rewarded with cryptocurrency (Any et al., 2024). While PoW is secure and reliable, its high energy consumption and scalability issues have led to the development of alternative mechanisms.

PoS: PoS is a more energy-efficient alternative to PoW. In PoS, validators are chosen based on the number of coins they hold and are willing to "stake" as collateral. This mechanism reduces the computational effort required to validate transactions and is considered more scalable (Huseynov and Mitchell, 2024). Ethereum 2.0, for example, has transitioned from PoW to PoS to improve scalability and reduce energy consumption.

Delegated PoS (DPoS): DPoS is a variation of PoS where stakeholders elect a small number of delegates to validate transactions and create new blocks on their behalf. This approach, used by networks like EOS, aims to increase efficiency and speed while maintaining decentralization (Awerika et al., 2023).

Blockchain technology offers numerous opportunities to enhance and streamline operations in the tourism and hospitality sectors. From booking systems to payment processing, identity verification, and supply chain management, blockchain can address several challenges faced by these industries. One of the most significant applications of blockchain in tourism and hospitality is in booking systems. Traditional booking systems are often centralized and involve multiple intermediaries, leading to increased costs and potential inefficiencies. Blockchain can streamline this process by providing a decentralized platform where hotels, airlines, and other service providers can interact directly with customers.

Blockchain-based booking systems can eliminate intermediaries, reducing costs for both service providers and customers. They also enhance transparency, as all transactions are recorded on the blockchain and are visible to all participants. This transparency can help prevent issues such as double bookings and ensure that customers get what they pay for (Edastama et al., 2021). Furthermore, smart contracts, which are self-executing contracts with the terms directly written into code, can automate booking processes. For example, a smart contract could automatically confirm a hotel reservation once the payment is made, streamlining the process and reducing the risk of human error.

Blockchain's secure and efficient payment processing capabilities make it an ideal solution for the tourism and hospitality industries. Traditional payment methods, especially those involving international transactions, often come with high fees and lengthy processing times. Blockchain can address these issues by enabling fast, secure, and low-cost payments through cryptocurrencies and digital assets. Cryptocurrencies such as Bitcoin and Ethereum can facilitate instant cross-border transactions without the need for intermediaries like banks. This capability is particularly beneficial in the tourism industry, where customers often make international payments for travel bookings and services (Lutfiani et al., 2022).

Additionally, blockchain's transparency and security can reduce the risk of fraud in payment processing. Each transaction is recorded on the blockchain and cannot be altered, providing a clear and immutable record of all payments. Identity verification is a critical aspect of the tourism and hospitality sectors, particularly for activities like flight bookings, hotel check-ins, and car rentals. Blockchain can enhance the security and efficiency of identity verification processes by providing a decentralized and tamper-proof platform for storing and verifying identity information. With blockchain, travelers can store their identity information in a secure digital wallet and share it with service providers as needed. This approach can streamline check-in processes at hotels and airports, reduce waiting times, and enhance the overall customer experience (Any et al., 2024). Moreover, blockchain-based identity verification can help combat fraud and ensure the authenticity of identity documents. Since data on the blockchain is immutable and transparent, it is difficult for fraudsters to alter or fake identity information.

Supply chain management is another area where blockchain technology can bring significant improvements. The tourism and hospitality sectors rely on complex supply chains to deliver goods and services, from food and beverages to travel and accommodation services. Blockchain can provide a transparent and secure platform for tracking and managing these supply chains. By recording every transaction and movement of goods on the blockchain, stakeholders can gain real-time visibility into the supply chain. This transparency can help ensure the authenticity and quality of products, prevent counterfeiting, and streamline logistics processes (Huseynov and Mitchell, 2024). For example, a hotel chain could use blockchain to track the sourcing and delivery of food and beverages, ensuring that they meet quality standards and are delivered on time. Similarly, travel agencies could use blockchain to manage the supply of travel services, such as flights and accommodations, ensuring that they are delivered as promised.

Customer loyalty programs are widely used in the tourism and hospitality sectors to reward repeat customers and encourage brand loyalty. However, traditional loyalty programs often face challenges such as complex redemption processes, low participation rates, and limited interoperability across different service providers. Blockchain can address these challenges by providing a decentralized platform for managing loyalty programs. With blockchain, customers can earn and redeem loyalty points seamlessly across multiple service providers, enhancing the value and flexibility of loyalty programs (Edastama et al., 2021). For example, a customer could earn loyalty points for staying at a hotel and use those points to book a flight with a partner airline. Blockchain's transparency and security also help prevent fraud and ensure that loyalty points are accurately recorded and redeemed.

The tourism industry, a significant driver of global economic activity, faces numerous challenges and opportunities as it continues to evolve in the digital age. Blockchain technology, known for its decentralized, secure, and transparent nature, presents innovative solutions that can address these challenges and transform the industry. This exploration delves into the fundamental principles of blockchain, its key components, and how it can revolutionize various aspects of the tourism sector. The tourism industry is a vast and complex ecosystem encompassing transportation, accommodation, dining, and entertainment services. It is characterized by a diverse range of stakeholders, including travelers, service providers, travel agents, and regulatory

10 *The Future of Blockchain in Tourism and Hospitality*

bodies. In 2019, before the COVID-19 pandemic, international tourism generated $1.7 trillion in export earnings and accounted for 10% of global employment (World Tourism Organization, 2020).

The industry is marked by a myriad of players, including travel agents, booking platforms, hotels, and tour operators, each adding layers of complexity to the process of booking travel and accommodations. This fragmentation often results in inefficiencies and increased costs, as multiple intermediaries vie for their share of the market. Moreover, the lack of transparency and trust further compounds the industry's challenges. Consumers frequently encounter issues such as fraudulent bookings, hidden fees, and opaque pricing models, which erode trust and confidence in the travel experience. The opacity in transaction processes makes it challenging for travelers to ascertain the authenticity of services and products, leading to skepticism and apprehension. Another significant concern in the tourism industry pertains to data security and privacy. Given its heavy reliance on personal data for booking and identification purposes, the industry is increasingly vulnerable to cyber threats and breaches. The collection and storage of sensitive information raise valid concerns regarding data security and privacy, necessitating robust measures to safeguard against potential risks and breaches. Furthermore, navigating regulatory and compliance frameworks presents a formidable challenge for both travelers and service providers alike. With varying regulations and compliance requirements across different countries, ensuring adherence to legal standards can be a complex and arduous task. The intricacies of compliance not only pose logistical challenges but also entail substantial administrative burdens, potentially impeding the seamless functioning of the tourism ecosystem. In essence, addressing these challenges requires a concerted effort from industry stakeholders to streamline processes, enhance transparency, fortify data security measures, and navigate regulatory complexities effectively. By prioritizing these areas of concern and fostering collaboration and innovation, the tourism industry can overcome its challenges and pave the way for sustainable growth and development.

Blockchain technology, with its unique features of decentralization, transparency, security, and immutability, offers promising solutions to these challenges. Originally developed to support the cryptocurrency Bitcoin, blockchain has evolved into a versatile technology with applications far beyond digital currencies. Blockchain is a distributed ledger technology that records transactions across a

Blockchain in tourism and hospitality 11

network of computers, or "nodes." Each transaction is grouped into a "block," which is then linked to the previous block, forming a "chain" of blocks. This structure ensures that data is secure, transparent, and immutable (Treiblmaier and Önder, 2019). Blockchain technology has garnered significant attention for its revolutionary attributes, fundamentally altering traditional centralized systems.

At its core, decentralization is one of blockchain's defining features. In contrast to centralized systems where a single entity wields control over data, blockchain operates through a network of nodes, each maintaining an identical copy of the entire ledger. This distribution of control ensures that no single entity can manipulate the data or disrupt the system. By spreading data across multiple nodes, blockchain enhances resilience, mitigating the risk of attacks or failures that could cripple a centralized system. The transparency inherent in blockchain technology is another key aspect that sets it apart from conventional systems. Every transaction recorded on the blockchain is visible to all participants within the network. This transparency fosters trust among users, as they can independently verify transactions without relying on intermediaries. Unlike traditional financial systems where transaction records are often opaque, blockchain offers a clear and auditable trail of transactions, promoting accountability and reducing the potential for fraud or corruption. Security is paramount in any digital ecosystem, and blockchain addresses this need through sophisticated cryptographic techniques. Each block in the blockchain is linked to the preceding one through a cryptographic hash, creating a chain of blocks that is resistant to tampering. This cryptographic linkage ensures that altering data within a block would necessitate altering subsequent blocks, making it exceedingly difficult for malicious actors to manipulate the ledger without detection.

Furthermore, the decentralized nature of blockchain enhances security by eliminating single points of failure and reducing the risk of data breaches or cyberattacks. Immutability is a core principle underpinning blockchain technology, reinforcing the integrity and reliability of the data stored within the ledger. Once a transaction is recorded on the blockchain, it becomes immutable, meaning it cannot be altered or deleted. This feature provides a guarantee of data integrity, as participants can trust that the information stored on the blockchain is accurate and tamper-proof. Immutability is particularly valuable in applications such as supply chain management, where maintaining an

12   *The Future of Blockchain in Tourism and Hospitality*

unforgeable record of transactions is essential for ensuring product authenticity and tracing the origins of goods.

The integration of blockchain technology into the tourism industry represents a promising avenue for addressing existing challenges while unlocking new opportunities for innovation and efficiency. One key area where blockchain can make a significant impact is in streamlining booking processes. Traditionally, the tourism sector has relied heavily on intermediaries for booking and reservation systems, leading to higher costs and slower transaction times. By leveraging blockchain technology, these intermediaries can be eliminated or minimized, resulting in lower costs and faster transactions for both travelers and service providers. Moreover, blockchain's inherent characteristics, such as immutability and transparency, can greatly enhance trust within the tourism ecosystem. By providing a tamper-proof record of transactions, blockchain can instill confidence between travelers and service providers, thereby improving overall transparency and trust. For instance, travelers can verify the authenticity of bookings and transactions without relying on centralized authorities, leading to a more trustworthy and reliable booking experience. In addition to improving trust, blockchain technology offers robust security features that can address concerns related to data security and privacy in the tourism industry.

With the increasing prevalence of cyber threats and data breaches, safeguarding sensitive personal information has become paramount. Blockchain's decentralized nature and cryptographic protocols ensure that sensitive data remains secure and tamper-proof, thereby enhancing privacy for travelers and protecting against unauthorized access or manipulation of data. Furthermore, blockchain has the potential to simplify cross-border payments and compliance processes within the tourism sector. Given the global nature of the industry, navigating cross-border transactions and regulatory requirements can be complex and time-consuming. Blockchain provides a secure and transparent platform for conducting transactions, eliminating the need for intermediaries and reducing the associated costs and delays. Additionally, by automating compliance processes through smart contracts and immutable records, blockchain can streamline regulatory compliance, ensuring that transactions adhere to applicable laws and regulations across different jurisdictions.

In the following sections, we will explore these applications in greater detail, examining how blockchain technology can revolutionize various aspects of the tourism industry. Understanding the core components and features of blockchain technology is essential to appreciate its potential impact on the tourism industry. This section provides a detailed overview of these fundamentals and explores how they can be applied to address the specific challenges of tourism. Decentralization is one of the most transformative aspects of blockchain technology. In a decentralized network, control is distributed among all participants rather than being held by a single entity. This principle has profound implications for the tourism industry, where the centralization of services often leads to inefficiencies and increased costs. Traditional booking systems often involve multiple intermediaries, such as online travel agencies (OTAs), which charge significant fees and add layers of complexity to the process. A decentralized booking system, powered by blockchain, can connect travelers directly with service providers (Saulina and Delhi, 2024).

- **Lower Costs**: By eliminating intermediaries, decentralized booking systems can reduce transaction fees and lower the overall cost of booking travel and accommodations.
- **Faster Transactions**: Decentralized systems can process transactions more quickly by removing the need for third-party verification and approval.
- **Greater Control for Service Providers**: Service providers can manage their own listings and pricing directly, without relying on intermediaries. This autonomy can lead to more competitive pricing and better customer service.

Blockchain can facilitate the creation of P2P marketplaces in tourism, where travelers can directly exchange services and experiences. For example, a blockchain-based P2P platform could allow travelers to rent out their homes, cars, or equipment to other travelers without the need for a central authority (Huseynov and Mitchell, 2024).

- **Trust and Security**: Blockchain provides a secure and transparent platform for P2P transactions, ensuring that all parties can verify the authenticity of the services and trust the other participants.
- **Diverse and Unique Offerings**: P2P marketplaces can offer a wider range of unique and personalized travel experiences, as they are not limited by the offerings of traditional service providers.

14   *The Future of Blockchain in Tourism and Hospitality*

Transparency is crucial in building trust between travelers and service providers. Blockchain's transparent and immutable ledger can provide a reliable and verifiable record of transactions, enhancing trust in the tourism industry. One of the significant challenges in the tourism industry is the proliferation of fake reviews and ratings, which can mislead travelers and harm the reputation of legitimate businesses. Blockchain can address this issue by providing a transparent and verifiable platform for reviews and ratings (Treiblmaier and Önder, 2019).

- **Authentic Reviews**: Reviews and ratings recorded on the blockchain are linked to verified transactions, ensuring that only genuine customers can leave feedback.
- **Tamper-Proof Records**: Once recorded, reviews and ratings cannot be altered or deleted, providing a permanent and trustworthy record.
- **Enhanced Credibility**: The transparency and authenticity of blockchain-based reviews can enhance the credibility of businesses and build trust among travelers.

Hidden fees and opaque pricing models are common issues in the tourism industry, leading to frustration and mistrust among travelers. Blockchain can provide a transparent and immutable record of all transactions, ensuring that pricing and fees are clear and verifiable (Lui et al., 2023).

- **Clear and Transparent Pricing**: Blockchain can record the entire transaction history, including all fees and charges, providing a clear and transparent view of the total cost.
- **Fair and Consistent Pricing**: The transparency of blockchain can prevent price manipulation and ensure that all travelers receive fair and consistent pricing.

The tourism industry relies heavily on personal data for booking and identification purposes, making data security and privacy critical concerns. Blockchain's robust security features can protect sensitive data and ensure the privacy of travelers. Blockchain can provide a secure and decentralized platform for storing personal data, reducing the risk of data breaches and unauthorized access (Fahmi et al., 2023).

Decentralized data storage is a fundamental concept in blockchain technology, revolutionizing traditional centralized systems. In a centralized system, data is stored in a single location, making it vulnerable to attacks and compromises. However, with blockchain, data is distributed across a network of nodes, each maintaining a copy of the entire database. This distribution ensures redundancy and resilience, as there is no single point of failure. Moreover, the decentralized nature of blockchain makes it inherently resistant to censorship and tampering, as altering data in one node would require altering the majority of nodes in the network simultaneously, which is practically impossible. One of the key pillars of blockchain security is encryption and cryptography. Blockchain utilizes advanced cryptographic techniques to secure data, transactions, and communications within the network. Each transaction is cryptographically linked to the previous one, forming an immutable chain of blocks. Additionally, public-key cryptography is employed to authenticate users and ensure that only authorized parties can access and interact with the blockchain. This robust encryption ensures the integrity and confidentiality of data, safeguarding it against unauthorized access and manipulation. Furthermore, blockchain has the potential to revolutionize identity management through self-sovereign identity systems. In traditional identity systems, individuals often lack control over their personal data, which is stored and managed by centralized authorities. However, with self-sovereign identity on the blockchain, individuals have full ownership and control over their identity information. They can choose what data to disclose, whom to share it with, and for what purposes. By leveraging blockchain's decentralized architecture and cryptographic security, self-sovereign identity systems empower individuals to manage their digital identities autonomously, reducing the risks of identity theft, fraud, and privacy breaches.

Blockchain can enhance the security of payment systems in the tourism industry by providing a secure and transparent platform for transactions (Awerika et al., 2023).

- **Secure Transactions**: Blockchain's cryptographic techniques ensure that transactions are secure and cannot be altered or forged.
- **Reduced Fraud**: The transparency and immutability of blockchain can prevent fraudulent transactions and protect both travelers and service providers from scams.

16 *The Future of Blockchain in Tourism and Hospitality*

- **Simplified Cross-Border Payments**: Blockchain can simplify cross-border payments by providing a single, secure platform for transactions, reducing the need for multiple intermediaries and currency conversions.

Blockchain's immutability ensures that once data is recorded, it cannot be altered or deleted. This feature is particularly valuable for compliance and regulatory purposes in the tourism industry. Blockchain can provide a transparent and immutable record of all transactions, simplifying compliance and regulatory reporting for tourism businesses (Handayani et al., 2023).

- **Accurate and Verifiable Records**: Blockchain provides a permanent and tamper-proof record of all transactions, ensuring that businesses can easily verify and report their activities.
- **Simplified Auditing**: The transparency and immutability of blockchain can simplify the auditing process, reducing the time and cost associated with compliance.
- **Enhanced Accountability**: Blockchain's transparent and immutable ledger can enhance accountability, ensuring that businesses adhere to regulatory requirements and industry standards.

Navigating different regulatory frameworks and compliance requirements across various countries can be complex and challenging for the tourism industry. Blockchain can simplify cross-border compliance by providing a single, transparent platform for transactions (Zwitter and Hazenberg, 2020).

Blockchain technology has emerged as a promising solution for enhancing various aspects of the tourism industry, primarily due to its ability to provide consistent and transparent records of transactions across different jurisdictions. By leveraging blockchain, tourism businesses can establish a reliable and immutable ledger that tracks every transaction, reservation, and payment made within the industry. This transparency not only simplifies the compliance process but also fosters trust among stakeholders, including travelers, service providers, and regulatory authorities. Furthermore, blockchain facilitates streamlined documentation and reporting procedures in tourism. Traditional methods of managing documentation and compliance often involve cumbersome paperwork, manual verification processes, and potential errors. With blockchain, these processes can be automated and standardized, reducing the administrative burden and complexity associated with cross-border operations.

By digitizing and securely storing essential documents, such as visas, permits, and contracts, blockchain enables tourism businesses to operate more efficiently while ensuring compliance with regulatory requirements. Moreover, the transparency and immutability inherent in blockchain technology can foster international cooperation and coordination within the tourism sector. In an increasingly interconnected world, where travelers often cross multiple borders during their journeys, maintaining consistency and compliance with global standards is paramount. Blockchain facilitates real-time access to accurate and verifiable data, enabling businesses to demonstrate their adherence to regulatory frameworks across jurisdictions. This transparency not only enhances trust between different stakeholders but also promotes collaboration among governments, industry associations, and international organizations in setting and enforcing standards for responsible tourism practices.

The application of blockchain technology in the tourism industry spans various sectors and services. This section explores several key use cases, illustrating how blockchain can transform different aspects of the industry. One of the most significant applications of blockchain in tourism is in the area of travel booking and reservations. Blockchain can streamline the booking process, reduce costs, and enhance the overall experience for travelers. Traditional travel booking platforms often rely on multiple intermediaries, leading to higher costs and inefficiencies. Blockchain can facilitate the development of decentralized travel booking platforms that connect travelers directly with service providers (Saulina and Delhi, 2024).

- **Direct Connections**: Decentralized platforms eliminate the need for intermediaries, allowing travelers to book directly with hotels, airlines, and other service providers.
- **Lower Fees**: By removing intermediaries, decentralized platforms can reduce transaction fees and lower the overall cost of bookings.
- **Enhanced Transparency**: Blockchain's transparent and immutable ledger provides a clear record of all transactions, ensuring that pricing and fees are transparent and verifiable.

Smart contracts are self-executing contracts with the terms of the agreement directly written into code. They can automate and

18 *The Future of Blockchain in Tourism and Hospitality*

streamline the booking process, reducing the need for manual intervention and ensuring that all parties fulfill their obligations (Lutfiani et al., 2022).

- **Automated Transactions**: Smart contracts can automatically execute and verify transactions, ensuring that bookings are processed quickly and accurately.
- **Conditional Payments**: Smart contracts can facilitate conditional payments, where funds are only released when specific conditions are met, such as the traveler checking into a hotel.
- **Reduced Disputes**: The automation and transparency of smart contracts can reduce the likelihood of disputes and ensure that all parties adhere to the agreed terms.

In recent years, identity verification and management have emerged as critical concerns within the tourism industry, particularly concerning international travel. With the increasing complexity and risks associated with identity-related issues, the need for a secure and efficient platform for managing and verifying identities has become apparent. Blockchain technology has been proposed as a potential solution to address these challenges effectively (Any et al., 2024).

One significant advantage of utilizing blockchain for identity management in the tourism sector is the provision of secure and verifiable identities. Through the implementation of digital passports and identity tokens stored securely on the blockchain, travelers can ensure the accuracy and integrity of their identity information (Any et al., 2024). The tamper-proof nature of blockchain technology offers a robust layer of security, safeguarding sensitive data against unauthorized access or manipulation. Moreover, blockchain has the potential to simplify the verification process for travelers and service providers alike. By streamlining identity verification procedures, blockchain enables travelers to share their identity information seamlessly with airlines, hotels, and other relevant entities (Any et al., 2024). This streamlined approach enhances operational efficiency and improves the overall travel experience by reducing wait times and administrative burdens at various touchpoints. Additionally, the adoption of blockchain technology in identity management offers enhanced privacy protections for travelers. With blockchain, individuals retain control over their identity information and can selectively share data with trusted parties as needed (Any et al., 2024). This empowerment

Blockchain in tourism and hospitality 19

ensures that travelers' privacy rights are respected while still facilitating necessary interactions with service providers throughout their journey.

Furthermore, the application of blockchain extends beyond identity management to revolutionize border control and immigration processes within the tourism industry. By providing a secure and transparent platform for managing immigration and customs data, blockchain accelerates the processing of travelers at border checkpoints (Nagel and Kranz, 2020). This efficiency not only enhances security measures but also contributes to reducing wait times and congestion, thereby improving the overall travel experience. The immutable and transparent nature of blockchain technology enhances security by ensuring the accuracy and verifiability of identity information (Nagel and Kranz, 2020). This resilience against tampering or fraudulent activities strengthens border control mechanisms and mitigates risks associated with identity fraud or unauthorized entry. Moreover, blockchain's capacity to facilitate fast and secure transactions has significant implications for payment systems and currency exchange in the tourism sector. Cryptocurrencies operating on blockchain technology, such as Bitcoin and Ethereum, offer a convenient and secure alternative for travelers to make payments (Treiblmaier and Önder, 2019). These digital currencies enable quick and secure transactions without the need for intermediaries like banks or payment processors.

Furthermore, the adoption of cryptocurrencies in the tourism industry presents opportunities for reduced transaction fees, especially for cross-border payments (Treiblmaier and Önder, 2019). By bypassing traditional financial intermediaries, cryptocurrency transactions often incur lower fees, translating into cost savings for travelers. This affordability enhances the accessibility of financial services for individuals traveling internationally, irrespective of geographical barriers or currency disparities. Additionally, cryptocurrencies' global acceptance facilitates seamless cross-border payments, providing a consistent and convenient payment method for travelers worldwide (Treiblmaier and Önder, 2019). The decentralized nature of blockchain ensures that transactions can be executed seamlessly across various jurisdictions, eliminating the complexities associated with traditional payment systems. Furthermore, blockchain technology simplifies currency exchange processes, offering a transparent and efficient platform for converting funds across different currencies (Huseynov and Mitchell, 2024). By leveraging blockchain

20 *The Future of Blockchain in Tourism and Hospitality*

for currency exchange, travelers can benefit from lower exchange fees and real-time transfer capabilities (Huseynov and Mitchell, 2024). These features enhance the efficiency of cross-border transactions and contribute to a more seamless travel experience for individuals navigating diverse financial landscapes.

Loyalty programs and rewards are an important aspect of the tourism industry, encouraging customer retention and repeat business. Blockchain can enhance the management and redemption of loyalty points, providing a more efficient and transparent platform for reward programs. Blockchain can enable the tokenization of loyalty points, allowing travelers to earn, transfer, and redeem points securely and efficiently (Asif and Hassan, 2023).

- **Interoperable Points**: Tokenized loyalty points can be used across different platforms and service providers, providing greater flexibility and convenience for travelers.
- **Secure and Transparent Transactions**: Blockchain provides a secure and transparent platform for managing loyalty points, ensuring that points are accurately recorded and easily verifiable.
- **Reduced Fraud**: The transparency and immutability of blockchain can prevent fraud and ensure that loyalty points are genuine and valid.

Blockchain can facilitate the development of decentralized loyalty platforms, where multiple service providers collaborate to offer integrated loyalty programs (Awerika et al., 2023).

- **Integrated Rewards**: Decentralized platforms allow travelers to earn and redeem loyalty points across different service providers, creating a seamless and integrated reward experience.
- **Greater Choice and Flexibility**: Travelers have more choices and flexibility in how they use their loyalty points, enhancing the overall value and appeal of reward programs.
- **Enhanced Customer Engagement**: Decentralized platforms can provide personalized and targeted rewards, enhancing customer engagement and satisfaction.

Blockchain can improve supply chain management in the tourism industry, providing transparency and traceability for the movement of goods and services. Blockchain can provide a transparent and immutable record of the entire supply chain, from the production of goods to their delivery to consumers (Lui et al., 2023).

- **Enhanced Visibility**: Blockchain provides a transparent view of the entire supply chain, allowing all participants to track the movement of goods and verify their authenticity.
- **Improved Efficiency**: Blockchain can streamline supply chain processes by providing a single, transparent platform for recording and managing transactions.
- **Reduced Fraud**: The transparency and immutability of blockchain can prevent fraud and ensure that all goods and services are genuine and traceable.

According to Awerika et al. (2023), blockchain offers robust cryptographic techniques that ensure the security of payments and transactions within the tourism sector. This heightened security is crucial in an industry where financial transactions and the exchange of sensitive customer data are commonplace. Furthermore, the transparency and immutability of blockchain contribute to reducing fraud within the tourism sector (Zwitter and Hazenberg, 2020). By providing a decentralized ledger where transactions can be tracked and verified, blockchain minimizes the risk of fraudulent activities, thereby bolstering trust among stakeholders. Moreover, blockchain simplifies the verification process for payments, ensuring that transactions are processed quickly and accurately (Huseynov and Mitchell, 2024). Through automation and the elimination of intermediaries, blockchain streamlines payment processes, leading to enhanced operational efficiency for businesses and improved customer experiences.

Despite these advantages, the integration of blockchain into the tourism industry is not without challenges. Scalability remains a significant concern, particularly in light of the industry's growing transaction volumes (Nagel and Kranz, 2020).

Blockchain networks may encounter bottlenecks when processing large volumes of transactions, impeding their ability to meet the demands of the tourism sector. Moreover, high transaction fees on some blockchain networks present a barrier to adoption, especially for low-value transactions (Handayani et al., 2023). These fees can deter businesses and consumers from utilizing blockchain-based payment solutions, hindering the technology's widespread implementation within the tourism industry.

22 *The Future of Blockchain in Tourism and Hospitality*

Interoperability between different blockchain platforms and traditional systems is also crucial for successful integration (Saulina and Delhi, 2024). Efforts to establish compatibility and standardization frameworks are necessary to facilitate seamless data exchange and communication between disparate systems (Fahmi et al., 2023). In conclusion, while blockchain holds promise for enhancing security and efficiency in the tourism industry, addressing technical challenges and ensuring interoperability with existing systems are essential for its successful implementation. By overcoming these obstacles, stakeholders can harness the full potential of blockchain technology to revolutionize payment and transaction processes, ultimately benefiting both businesses and travelers alike.

The regulatory and legal landscape for blockchain technology is still evolving, presenting several challenges for its implementation in the tourism industry. Navigating the regulatory requirements for blockchain technology can be complex, particularly in the tourism industry, where businesses operate across multiple jurisdictions (Nagel and Kranz, 2020).

- **Data Privacy**: Blockchain's immutable nature can conflict with data privacy regulations, such as the General Data Protection Regulation (GDPR), which requires the ability to delete personal data.
- **Anti-Money Laundering (AML) and Know Your Customer (KYC)**: Compliance with AML and KYC regulations is essential for businesses using blockchain for financial transactions, requiring robust identity verification and monitoring systems.
- **Cross-Border Regulations**: The global nature of the tourism industry requires businesses to comply with different regulatory frameworks across various countries, adding complexity to the implementation of blockchain solutions.

The legal status and framework for blockchain technology are still developing, presenting challenges for its adoption in the tourism industry (Zwitter and Hazenberg, 2020).

- **Smart Contract Legality**: The legal recognition and enforceability of smart contracts vary across jurisdictions, potentially impacting their use in the tourism industry.
- **Intellectual Property**: Blockchain's transparency and immutability can raise concerns about the protection and ownership of intellectual property and confidential information.

Blockchain in tourism and hospitality 23

- **Consumer Protection**: Ensuring consumer protection and addressing legal liabilities in the context of decentralized and peer-to-peer blockchain systems can be challenging.

The adoption and integration of blockchain technology in the tourism industry have been the subject of extensive research and discourse in recent years. Awerika et al. (2023) emphasize the importance of collaboration among stakeholders to facilitate this transition smoothly. They highlight the necessity for aligning interests and objectives, developing industry standards, and fostering cross-sector partnerships. Zwitter and Hazenberg (2020) contribute to the discussion by emphasizing the challenges posed by stakeholder alignment and the significance of establishing industry standards. Their insights underscore the complexities inherent in integrating blockchain solutions within the tourism sector and the need for cohesive efforts among diverse stakeholders. Huseynov and Mitchell (2024) further explore the challenges faced by businesses in adopting blockchain technology, focusing on organizational readiness, legacy system integration, and user adoption. Their findings underscore the multifaceted nature of the transition process and the importance of addressing various hurdles to ensure successful implementation. Nagel and Kranz (2020) provide insights into the potential benefits of blockchain technology in tourism, highlighting its capacity to enhance transparency, security, and efficiency in various aspects of the industry. Their research underscores the transformative potential of blockchain solutions in revolutionizing traditional tourism processes and practices. Fahmi et al. (2023) delve into the intricacies of cross-sector partnerships and collaboration, emphasizing their role in driving innovation and fostering synergies across different industries. Their study highlights the value of interdisciplinary approaches in harnessing the full potential of blockchain technology in tourism and beyond.

Saulina and Delhi (2024) offer valuable insights into the challenges confronted by businesses during the transition to blockchain technology. From organizational readiness to legacy system integration and user adoption, their research sheds light on the complexities involved in this transformative process. Treiblmaier and Önder (2019) and Asif and Hassan (2023) contribute to the discourse by examining various aspects of blockchain technology and its implications for the tourism industry. Their studies offer valuable perspectives on the potential applications, benefits, and challenges associated with blockchain adoption in tourism. Lui et al. (2023) and Edastama et al.

24   *The Future of Blockchain in Tourism and Hospitality*

(2021) further enrich the discussion by exploring specific use cases and implementation strategies for blockchain technology in tourism. Their research provides practical insights and recommendations for businesses looking to leverage blockchain solutions to enhance their operations and services. Overall, these studies underscore the significance of collaboration, innovation, and strategic planning in driving the successful adoption and integration of blockchain technology in the tourism industry. By addressing challenges and leveraging opportunities, stakeholders can unlock the transformative potential of blockchain to revolutionize traditional tourism processes and deliver enhanced experiences for travelers.

The integration of blockchain technology in the tourism industry has garnered significant attention from scholars in recent years. Awerika et al. (2023) delve into the potential of blockchain to revolutionize various aspects of tourism, including data management and security. Similarly, Zwitter and Hazenberg (2020) explore the intersection of blockchain and tourism, shedding light on its implications for enhancing trust and transparency within the sector. In the pursuit of inclusive blockchain solutions, Huseynov and Mitchell (2024) emphasize the importance of addressing the digital divide and ensuring accessibility for all stakeholders. Their research underscores the need for user-friendly interfaces and equitable access to blockchain-based platforms. Nagel and Kranz (2020) further contribute to this discourse by examining the role of blockchain in promoting sustainability and social responsibility in tourism practices. Fahmi et al. (2023) highlight the ethical considerations inherent in blockchain adoption within the tourism industry. Their work underscores the significance of data ownership, transparency, and ethical data use in safeguarding individual privacy rights. Building upon this, Saulina and Delhi (2024) explore the broader social impact of blockchain technology, advocating for its alignment with sustainability and equity goals. Handayani et al. (2023) delve into the practical implications of integrating blockchain into tourism operations, emphasizing the need for robust governance frameworks and stakeholder engagement.

Treiblmaier and Önder (2019) contribute valuable insights into the technological aspects of blockchain implementation, offering guidance on optimizing its efficiency and scalability. Asif and Hassan (2023) explore the role of blockchain in enhancing customer experiences and streamlining transaction processes within the tourism sector. Their research underscores the potential of blockchain to drive innovation and value creation for both businesses and travelers. Lui et al. (2023) complement this perspective by examining the economic implications of blockchain adoption in tourism, highlighting its potential to generate new revenue streams and unlock market efficiencies. Edastama et al. (2021) offer a comprehensive overview of blockchain applications in tourism, synthesizing insights from various disciplines to elucidate its multifaceted impact. Their work serves as a valuable resource for policymakers, industry practitioners, and researchers seeking to navigate the complexities of blockchain integration in the tourism landscape. Overall, these scholarly contributions collectively enrich our understanding of the opportunities and challenges associated with blockchain technology in reshaping the future of tourism.

The integration of blockchain technology into the tourism industry is still in its early stages, but it offers significant opportunities for innovation and transformation. This section explores the future outlook for blockchain in tourism and identifies potential opportunities for growth and development. One of the key trends shaping the future of blockchain technology in the tourism industry is the development of decentralized travel ecosystems (Saulina and Delhi, 2024). These ecosystems involve multiple stakeholders collaborating on a shared blockchain platform to streamline processes and enhance the overall travel experience. Decentralized ecosystems have the potential to integrate various services, such as booking, payments, and loyalty programs, into a seamless and cohesive experience for consumers (Awerika et al., 2023). By leveraging blockchain technology, these ecosystems can offer greater efficiency and transparency in transactions, leading to improved trust among stakeholders (Huseynov and Mitchell, 2024). Moreover, collaborative platforms enabled by blockchain facilitate cooperation among different service providers, allowing them to share resources and data to offer more integrated solutions to travelers (Nagel and Kranz, 2020). Another emerging trend in the integration of blockchain technology in the tourism industry is its combination with the Internet of Things (IoT) (Handayani et al., 2023). This integration opens up new possibilities for enhancing the travel experience through smart tourism solutions. By connecting devices and sensors via blockchain networks, smart tourism solutions can provide real-time data and insights to travelers, enabling them to make more informed decisions and enjoy a more immersive travel experience (Fahmi et al., 2023). The integration of

26 *The Future of Blockchain in Tourism and Hospitality*

blockchain and IoT also offers benefits in terms of data management and security (Lui et al., 2023).

Blockchain provides a secure and transparent platform for managing and sharing data from IoT devices, ensuring the integrity and accuracy of the information. This enhanced data security is particularly important in the tourism industry, where sensitive personal and financial information is exchanged between travelers and service providers (Edastama et al., 2021). By leveraging blockchain technology, the tourism industry can mitigate the risks associated with data breaches and unauthorized access, thereby enhancing trust and confidence among travelers. Moreover, the combination of blockchain and IoT enables personalized experiences for travelers based on real-time data and insights from connected devices (Treiblmaier and Önder, 2019). By analyzing data such as location, preferences, and behavior patterns, tourism businesses can tailor their services to meet the individual needs and preferences of travelers (Asif and Hassan, 2023). This personalized approach not only enhances the overall travel experience but also fosters greater loyalty and satisfaction among customers, ultimately driving business growth and success. In conclusion, the integration of blockchain technology into the tourism industry holds immense potential for innovation and transformation. Decentralized travel ecosystems and the combination of blockchain and IoT are just some of the emerging trends shaping the future of tourism. By embracing these technologies, tourism businesses can unlock new opportunities for collaboration, efficiency, and personalization, ultimately delivering enhanced value to travelers and driving industry growth and development.

Blockchain technology offers significant opportunities for growth and development in the tourism industry, particularly in the areas of innovation, efficiency, and customer experience. Blockchain can drive innovation and enable the development of new business models in the tourism industry (Treiblmaier and Önder, 2019).

- **P2P Platforms**: Blockchain can facilitate the development of P2P platforms, where travelers can directly exchange services and experiences without the need for intermediaries.
- **Tokenized Economies**: The tokenization of assets and services on the blockchain can enable new economic models, where travelers can earn, trade, and redeem tokens for various goods and services.

Blockchain in tourism and hospitality 27

- **Decentralized Applications (DApps)**: Blockchain supports the development of decentralized applications (DApps) that deliver secure and transparent solutions across various sectors. By leveraging the decentralized nature of blockchain, DApps facilitate innovative processes such as booking and payments., ensuring that transactions are verified and recorded on distributed ledgers without the need for a central authority.

Key features and principles

Blockchain technology's most essential feature is decentralization, distinguishing it from traditional centralized systems in which a single entity controls the entire database. In blockchain networks, the database is distributed among a vast network of nodes, each maintaining a copy of the entire blockchain (Treiblmaier and Önder, 2019). This decentralized structure effectively eradicates any single point of control or potential failure. Even if some nodes in the network become compromised, the system's robustness remains unaltered, ensuring continuous operation (Lutfiani et al., 2022). The decentralized architecture of blockchain enhances not only the system's reliability but also its security. In contrast to centralized systems, where hacking or central server failures can bring the entire system down, a blockchain network can maintain its functionality even if multiple nodes are attacked or go offline (Any et al., 2024). This resilience is crucial in industries where data security and system uptime are vital, such as finance, healthcare, and supply chains (Saulina and Delhi, 2024).

Furthermore, the decentralized nature of blockchain promotes greater transparency, which is essential for building trust among users. In centralized systems, data and transactions are often controlled by a single entity, which can result in opacity and mistrust (Lui et al., 2023). With blockchain, all transactions are recorded on a public ledger, enabling every participant to view and independently verify the authenticity of transactions. This transparency enhances trust and accountability, making blockchain a reliable choice for various applications (Edastama et al., 2021; Zwitter and Hazenberg, 2020).

Decentralization in blockchain offers several advantages; one is empowering users by democratizing data control. In traditional centralized systems, power and control are typically concentrated in the hands of a central authority, which can lead to issues of censorship, bias, and unequal access. In contrast, blockchain networks distribute control among all participants, reducing the risk of these problems and encouraging a more equitable system. This fair and decentralized approach allows each participant to have an equal role in the network's operation, leading to more democratic decision-making processes and increased fairness (Huseynov and Mitchell, 2024). Furthermore, decentralization fosters innovation by enabling more participants to contribute to the system's development and improvement (Saulina and Delhi, 2024). With control not limited to a single entity, diverse developers from various backgrounds and perspectives can collaborate, driving innovation and technological advancements. This inclusive environment encourages the emergence of new ideas, ensuring blockchain technology remains at the forefront of innovation (Hoffman et al., 2020).

The transactional flow in blockchain technology is detailed in Figure 1.1. The fundamental component of the blockchain architecture is the node, which can be users or highly configured computers. These nodes play a crucial role in blockchain transactions and maintain a complete copy of the blockchain ledger, ensuring data redundancy and decentralization.

Nodes with special capabilities are known as miners, and these nodes have the capacity to add new blocks to the blockchain. Miners are responsible for the authentication, verification, and validation of

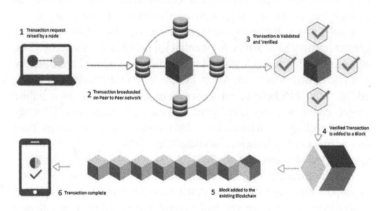

Figure 1.1 Transaction flow in blockchain technology.
Source: Singh et al. (2020).

transactions between both parties. Once a transaction is validated and authenticated by the miners, the amount is deducted from the sender's wallet and credited to the receiver's wallet. A block functions like a container that holds aggregated transaction details. When a new record or transaction is initiated in the blockchain, it results in the creation of a new block. These blocks can only be added to the blockchain after successful verification by miners. Each block consists of two main components: the header and the transaction details. The header includes the block version number, previous hash value, timestamp, Merkle root hash value, difficulty target value, nonce, and the block's hash value. The block version number is a 4-byte sequential identifier for the block. The previous hash value is the 256-bit hash result of all the transactions in the previous block, including its header, which helps link consecutive blocks. The timestamp, which is 4 bytes in size, indicates when the block was created. The Merkle root hash value is a 32-byte hash representing all the transactions arranged in a Merkle or binary tree structure. The difficulty target value, which is 4 bytes, specifies the required difficulty level for the PoW for the block. The nonce is a 32-bit random number that miners adjust to generate a unique hash value for the block that meets the PoW criteria.

When miners successfully find the correct nonce and the unique hash value for the block, they are rewarded, and the block is added to the blockchain. If an attacker modifies any transaction, the unique hash value of that block also changes. Additionally, this unique hash is linked to the next block's previous hash value. Once the nonce value is successfully varied and the unique hash of the block is found, the miner is rewarded, and the block is added to the blockchain. Figure 1.2 shows the linkage of two blocks based on their hash values.

The most defining characteristic of blockchain technology is its transparency, which promotes openness and trust within the network. Unlike traditional systems where transactions are opaque, blockchain allows all participants to seamlessly view and verify transactions (Handayani et al., 2023). Once a transaction is recorded on the blockchain, it becomes visible to every node in the network, allowing participants to confirm its authenticity and integrity, preventing unauthorized alterations independently. This unprecedented transparency instills confidence in users, assuring them that transactions are executed accurately and fairly (Nagel and Kranz, 2020). The block header comprises several critical components: the block version number, previous hash value, timestamp, Merkle root hash value,

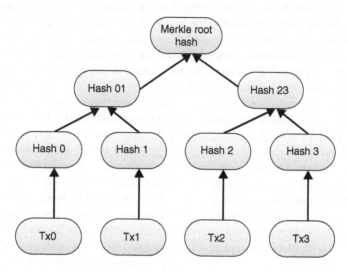

Figure 1.2 Calculation of Merkle root hash.

Source: Sonkor and De Soto (2022).

difficulty target value, nonce, and the block's hash value. The block version number is a 4-byte sequential identifier for the block. The previous hash is a 256-bit hash value derived from all transactions in the preceding block, including its header, which facilitates the linking of consecutive blocks. The timestamp, indicating when the block was created, is also 4 bytes in size. The Merkle root hash, a 32-byte hash value, represents all transactions arranged in a Merkle or binary tree structure. The difficulty target value, which is 4 bytes, specifies the required difficulty level for the PoW for the block (Awerika et al., 2023). The nonce is a 32-bit number that miners adjust to generate a unique hash value for the block that meets the PoW criteria. The unique hash value of the block, which miners aim to discover by varying the nonce, is the hash of the entire block. If a transaction is altered by an attacker, the unique hash value of the block changes as well (Lui et al., 2023). This unique hash is also linked to the next block's previous hash value. When a miner successfully finds the correct nonce and unique hash for the block, they are rewarded, and the block is added to the blockchain.

Blockchain in tourism and hospitality 31

The transparent nature of blockchain technology eliminates the need for a central authority to control the flow of information, thus removing concerns about the honesty and integrity of a controlling entity (Hoffman et al., 2020; Zwitter and Hazenberg, 2020). By recording transactions on a public ledger, blockchain allows any participant access to verify the accuracy of the data, thereby increasing trust and accountability. Its decentralized and distributed structure makes it extremely difficult for malicious entities to tamper with data undetected, ensuring robust security and data integrity (Saulina and Delhi, 2024).

The transparency of blockchain technology is essential in industries where trust and transparency are paramount, such as finance, supply chain management, and healthcare (Any et al., 2024). The accessibility and immutability of blockchain's public ledger create a more secure and accountable environment, reducing the risk of fraud, corruption, and unethical practices. As a result, organizations in these sectors are increasingly adopting blockchain technology to optimize their operations, governance, and compliance (Edastama et al., 2021).

In accountability, blockchain technology emerges as a beacon of transparency, pushing participants to behave more responsibly. Every maneuver etched into the blockchain is open to scrutiny, discouraging any dalliance with unethical practices as the specter of exposure looms large (Huseynov and Mitchell, 2024). This paradigm shift has profound implications for businesses, encouraging increased governance, enhanced compliance, and unwavering adherence to ethical precepts as companies come to terms with maintaining a transparent and reputable image (Lui et al., 2023). Furthermore, the transparency inherent in blockchain technology fosters a culture of collaboration and efficiency among stakeholders. As a single repository of truth, it allows all parties equal access to relevant data, reducing the risk of misunderstanding and conflict (Awerika et al., 2023). This democratization of information streamlines operations and enhances coordination, especially in complex supply chains where myriad entities must synchronize their efforts to monitor and validate the flow of goods and resources (Handayani et al., 2023). By providing an indelible ledger of transactions, blockchain technology paves the way for a smoother, more agile supply chain, reducing delays and improving overall performance.

32 *The Future of Blockchain in Tourism and Hospitality*

Blockchain technology prides itself on advanced security features, using complex cryptographic methods to ensure data integrity and confidentiality. Each transaction is encrypted and linked to the previous one, forming a complex chain of blocks resistant to tampering (Handayani et al., 2023). The cryptographic links between blocks ensure that changing a transaction requires changing all subsequent blocks, a challenging task due to the blockchain's intricate and decentralized structure (Lui et al., 2023). At the core of blockchain security is cryptographic hashing, which generates a unique string of characters, known as a hash, from transaction data. This hash is highly sensitive to tampering, producing very different outputs for even small changes in the input data. Each block in the blockchain contains its hash and the previous block's hash, creating a secure chain of blocks (Fahmi et al., 2023). To tamper with a single block, an attacker must modify that block and all subsequent blocks throughout the network, a formidable challenge due to the decentralized nature of the blockchain (Vasani et al., 2024). In addition, blockchain technologies use public and private keys to authenticate and authorize transactions. Each user has a unique public key, which serves as an address for receiving transactions, and a private key, kept confidential and used to sign transactions to verify the user's identity and consent. This dual-key system ensures that only the legitimate owner of the private key can initiate a transaction, providing an additional layer of security (Fahmi et al., 2023).

Blockchain technology offers a complex structure made up of many different components. To better understand this structure, we can look at its four key components: shared data, protocols, platforms, and products. Shared data, the foundation of blockchain, stores all transactions securely and transparently. This data is organized into blocks, and each block is associated with the hash value of the previous block. This creates a chain-like structure. This structure ensures that transactions are immutable and secure, because a change in any block leaves a trace throughout the chain. Another component that makes blockchain work is protocols. Protocols define the rules that apply to all participants in the blockchain network. These rules govern consensus mechanisms, i.e. how all participants in the network agree on the correctness of a transaction. In addition, these rules provide different incentives for participants and make it easier for new users to join the network. For example, the Bitcoin protocol offers rewards for adding new blocks through mining. Platforms provide

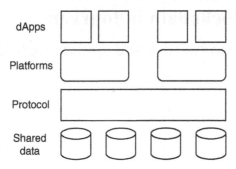

Figure 1.3 Different components of the blockchain technology stack.

Source: Singh et al. (2022).

the underlying infrastructure on which blockchain technology is built. These platforms allow developers to create various applications and services. Popular blockchain platforms, such as Ethereum, provide powerful tools for developing and executing smart contracts. The platforms provide an ecosystem where users can deploy these applications, providing the flexibility and functionality needed to realize the potential of blockchain technology. Finally, products are the applications and services that users interact with directly. These products offer innovative solutions in a variety of areas that leverage the security, transparency, and decentralization benefits of blockchain. Many different products, such as cryptocurrency wallets, digital identity management applications, or smart contract-based marketplaces, can be developed on blockchain platforms and used by users (see Figure 1.3).

2 Blockchain in tourism
Opportunities and applications

Overview of the global tourism industry

The global tourism industry plays a critical role in economic expansion, acting as a key driver of economic growth, job creation, and international understanding through various leisure, business, and cultural exploration activities. This sector contributes significantly to the global gross domestic product (GDP), fosters cross-cultural connections, and facilitates international collaboration and exchange (Prados-Castillo et al., 2023). This chapter delves into the multifaceted nature of the tourism industry, exploring the impacts of digital transformation, the rise of sustainability, experiential travel trends, and the influence of remote work. Tourism is one of the largest industries globally, contributing extensively to economic development. According to the World Travel and Tourism Council (WTTC), the tourism sector accounted for 10.4% of the global GDP and created 319 million jobs, or 10% of total employment, in 2018. The industry's economic influence extends beyond direct revenue from travel and hospitality services, impacting sectors such as retail, entertainment, and transportation. This multiplier effect highlights the tourism sector's pivotal role in the broader economic landscape (WTTC, 2019).

The advent of the digital age has revolutionized the tourism landscape, integrating technology to introduce personalized experiences, immersive virtual tours, and secure transactions. Digital platforms and tools have reshaped the way travelers plan, book, and experience their journeys. The increasing adoption of technologies such as artificial intelligence (AI), blockchain, and the Internet of Things (IoT) is driving the evolution of the industry to meet changing consumer demands. AI and big data analytics are transforming the travel

DOI: 10.4324/9781003521617-3

Blockchain in tourism: Opportunities and applications 35

experience by offering personalized recommendations and services. Companies like Google and Airbnb use algorithms to analyze user data and preferences, providing customized travel itineraries, accommodation suggestions, and activity recommendations. This level of personalization enhances customer satisfaction and loyalty (Treiblmaier and Önder, 2019).

Virtual reality (VR) and augmented reality (AR) technologies are offering new ways for travelers to explore destinations before they visit. These immersive experiences allow potential tourists to virtually tour hotels, landmarks, and attractions, aiding in decision-making and increasing engagement. Museums and historical sites have also adopted AR to provide enriched, interactive experiences for visitors (Erceg et al., 2020). Blockchain technology is revolutionizing the security and transparency of transactions in the tourism sector. By providing a decentralized and immutable ledger, blockchain ensures secure and efficient payment processing, identity verification, and contract management. This technology reduces fraud and enhances trust between stakeholders (Ozdemir et al., 2020). AI-powered chatbots and virtual assistants are streamlining the booking process, offering 24/7 support and handling complex queries with ease. These tools enhance the user experience by providing instant assistance and reducing wait times, thereby increasing conversion rates for travel companies (Erceg et al., 2020).

Sustainability has emerged as a significant trend in the tourism industry, driven by increasing environmental concerns and ethical considerations. Travelers are becoming more conscious of their environmental footprint and are opting for eco-friendly accommodations, responsible tourism practices, and support for local communities. Hotels and resorts are adopting sustainable practices such as using renewable energy, reducing water consumption, and minimizing waste. Certifications like LEED (Leadership in Energy and Environmental Design) and Green Key are helping travelers identify eco-friendly options. These initiatives not only appeal to environmentally conscious travelers but also contribute to the preservation of natural resources (Ratna et al., 2024). Responsible tourism emphasizes minimizing negative social, economic, and environmental impacts while maximizing benefits for local communities. This approach encourages travelers to respect local cultures, support local economies, and contribute to conservation efforts. Examples include

36 *The Future of Blockchain in Tourism and Hospitality*

community-based tourism initiatives and wildlife conservation projects (Zhang et al., 2023).

Travelers are increasingly interested in authentic cultural experiences that support local communities. This trend is leading to the rise of homestays, local tours, and community-run enterprises. By directly engaging with locals and contributing to their economies, tourists can ensure that their spending benefits those most in need (Ovezik et al., 2024). The trend toward experiential travel represents a shift in priorities, with travelers seeking authentic, meaningful experiences over material possessions. This type of travel is characterized by immersive cultural exchanges and transformative encounters with local communities. Experiential travel often involves deep cultural immersion, where travelers engage with local traditions, cuisines, and lifestyles. This can include participating in cooking classes, attending cultural festivals, or living with local families. Such experiences foster cross-cultural understanding and create lasting memories (Leible et al., 2019).

Travelers are increasingly looking for transformative experiences that offer personal growth and self-discovery. These encounters can range from adventure travel, such as trekking in remote regions, to wellness retreats focused on mental and physical health. The tourism industry is responding by offering curated itineraries that cater to these desires (Xu and Sun, 2024). The rise of remote work has given birth to a new demographic of travelers known as digital nomads. These individuals use technology to work remotely while exploring the world. The flexibility of remote work allows them to travel for extended periods, blending work and leisure in unique ways. For digital nomads, reliable internet connectivity is crucial. Destinations around the world are adapting by providing high-speed internet access in accommodations, cafes, and coworking spaces. Cities such as Bali, Chiang Mai, and Lisbon have become popular hubs for digital nomads due to their affordable living costs and robust digital infrastructure (Erceg et al., 2020). Coworking spaces are essential for digital nomads, offering a productive environment with all the necessary amenities. These spaces also provide opportunities for networking and collaboration, creating a sense of community among remote workers. The proliferation of coworking spaces in tourist destinations reflects the growing demand from this demographic (Treiblmaier and Önder, 2019).

Blockchain in tourism: Opportunities and applications 37

The future of travel is shaped by technological advancements, sustainability initiatives, experiential preferences, and changing work dynamics. Embracing these trends will allow the tourism industry to adapt to the evolving needs of travelers and provide sustainable and fulfilling travel experiences. The integration of advanced technologies such as AI, blockchain, VR, and AR will continue to transform the tourism industry. These technologies will enhance personalization, security, and engagement, creating a seamless and enriched travel experience. Future innovations may include AI-driven travel assistants that provide real-time updates and recommendations, as well as blockchain-based platforms that ensure transparent and secure transactions (Ratna et al., 2024). Sustainability will remain a central focus for the tourism industry. As environmental concerns grow, travelers will increasingly seek out eco-friendly options and responsible tourism practices. The industry must prioritize sustainable development, conservation efforts, and support for local communities to ensure long-term viability and appeal (Ovezik et al., 2024).

The trend toward experiential travel will continue to gain momentum, with travelers prioritizing authentic and meaningful experiences over material possessions. The industry will need to offer curated itineraries and unique cultural exchanges that cater to this demand. This shift in priorities will drive innovation in travel services and create opportunities for deeper engagement with local cultures (Xu and Sun, 2024). The rise of remote work and digital nomadism will shape the future of travel. Destinations will need to adapt by providing reliable internet connectivity, coworking spaces, and supportive communities for remote workers. This trend will create new opportunities for destinations to attract long-term visitors and foster economic growth through tourism (Treiblmaier and Önder, 2019). The global tourism industry is undergoing significant transformations driven by technological advancements, sustainability initiatives, experiential travel preferences, and changing work dynamics. By embracing these trends, the industry can adapt to the evolving needs of travelers and provide sustainable and fulfilling travel experiences. The integration of AI, blockchain, VR, and AR will enhance the travel journey, while a focus on sustainability and responsible tourism will ensure the preservation of destinations for future generations. The rise of digital nomads will create new opportunities for destinations to attract long-term visitors and drive economic growth. Ultimately, the future

38 *The Future of Blockchain in Tourism and Hospitality*

of travel lies in the industry's ability to innovate and respond to the changing landscape, ensuring a thriving and resilient tourism sector.

Challenges facing the tourism sector, including security, trust, and sustainability

The tourism industry, a cornerstone of global economic growth and cultural interaction, plays a vital role in connecting people across different geographies, fostering mutual understanding and cultural exchange. However, this sector is not without its challenges. Security risks, issues of trust, and sustainability concerns present significant hurdles that need addressing to ensure the continued prosperity and reputation of global tourism. This comprehensive analysis explores these challenges in detail, drawing from recent studies and reports to provide a nuanced understanding of the issues at hand. Security concerns, particularly those arising from terrorism and political unrest, pose formidable challenges to the tourism industry. Incidents of terrorism not only threaten the safety of travelers but also lead to economic losses and damage the reputation of affected destinations. For instance, the terrorist attacks in Paris in 2015 resulted in a significant decline in tourist arrivals, with the city's tourism revenue taking a substantial hit (Awerika et al., 2023). Similarly, political instability in regions such as the Middle East and North Africa has deterred tourists, leading to a downturn in tourism-dependent economies. The ramifications of such security threats are far-reaching. They can lead to a drop in international tourist arrivals, reduced investment in the tourism sector, and job losses, thereby affecting the overall economy. To mitigate these risks, it is essential for governments, destination authorities, and tourism stakeholders to collaborate effectively. This collaboration should focus on developing and implementing robust security measures that ensure a safe environment for travelers. Measures could include increased surveillance, improved security protocols at tourist sites, and the establishment of rapid response teams to address any security incidents promptly (Edastama et al., 2021).

Governments play a crucial role in safeguarding the tourism industry from security threats. National security policies must incorporate measures to protect tourists and tourism infrastructure. For example, the United States Department of State provides travel advisories to inform citizens of potential risks when traveling abroad, helping them make informed decisions (Edastama et al., 2021). Additionally, destination authorities need to work closely with local law enforcement and international security agencies to share intelligence and coordinate responses to potential threats. Tourism stakeholders, including businesses and service providers, also have a responsibility to ensure the safety of their patrons. Hotels, tour operators, and transportation companies should adopt best practices in security management, such as conducting regular security audits, training staff in emergency response procedures, and investing in security technologies like CCTV and biometric access control systems. By fostering a culture of safety and vigilance, the tourism sector can create a more secure environment for travelers.

Trust is the foundation upon which the tourism industry is built. Travelers entrust their well-being to service providers and destination authorities, expecting a safe and enjoyable experience. However, incidents such as scams, fraud, and safety lapses can quickly erode this trust. For instance, the prevalence of online booking scams, where travelers are defrauded by fake websites, has become a significant concern (Any et al., 2024). Similarly, incidents of food poisoning or accidents at tourist sites can damage the reputation of a destination and deter future visitors. To uphold and bolster trust, tourism stakeholders must prioritize transparency, ethical conduct, and accountability. Service providers should be transparent about their offerings, providing clear and accurate information to potential customers. Ethical conduct involves treating customers fairly and addressing their concerns promptly. Accountability means that businesses and authorities must take responsibility for any lapses in safety or service quality, implementing corrective measures and compensating affected individuals where necessary (Hoffman et al., 2020).

Safety protocols are essential for maintaining trust and ensuring the well-being of travelers. These protocols should cover various aspects of the tourism experience, from transportation and accommodation to activities and excursions. For example, hotels should have fire safety measures, such as smoke detectors, fire extinguishers, and clearly marked emergency exits. Tour operators should conduct thorough risk assessments for activities such as hiking, scuba diving, and safari tours, providing necessary safety equipment and trained guides. In the wake of the COVID-19 pandemic, hygiene and health safety have become paramount concerns for travelers. The tourism industry must adapt to these new expectations by implementing enhanced sanitation measures, such as regular cleaning of high-touch surfaces,

40   *The Future of Blockchain in Tourism and Hospitality*

providing hand sanitizers, and ensuring that staff follow health guidelines, including wearing masks and practicing social distancing (Hoffman et al., 2020). These measures not only protect travelers but also help restore confidence in the safety of travel. Open communication channels between service providers and travelers are crucial for addressing concerns and maintaining trust. Service providers should establish multiple channels for customers to reach out with questions, complaints, or feedback. These channels could include phone support, email, social media, and dedicated customer service platforms. Prompt and effective communication can help resolve issues quickly and prevent them from escalating into major problems. Moreover, destination authorities should engage with travelers through public information campaigns, providing updates on safety conditions, travel advisories, and any measures being taken to enhance security and safety. For instance, during a natural disaster or health crisis, timely and accurate information can help travelers make informed decisions and take necessary precautions (Hoffman et al., 2020).

The exponential growth of tourism has led to the phenomenon of over-tourism, where popular destinations become overwhelmed by the sheer number of visitors. This can result in environmental degradation, cultural exploitation, and strained local resources. Cities like Venice, Barcelona, and Dubrovnik have experienced the negative impacts of over-tourism, including pollution, damage to historical sites, and a decline in the quality of life for local residents (Nagel and Kranz, 2020). Over-tourism not only affects the environment and local communities but also diminishes the quality of the tourist experience. Crowded attractions, long wait times, and a lack of authentic cultural encounters can lead to visitor dissatisfaction and deter repeat visits. To address these issues, it is crucial for governments, businesses, and local communities to adopt sustainable tourism practices that balance the needs of tourists and the well-being of destinations.

Sustainable tourism involves minimizing the negative impacts of tourism on the environment and local communities while maximizing its economic and social benefits. This can be achieved through various strategies, such as promoting eco-friendly travel options, supporting local businesses, and encouraging responsible behavior among tourists. Governments and destination authorities can implement policies to manage visitor numbers and protect sensitive areas. For example, the introduction of visitor caps or timed entry systems at popular attractions can help control crowd sizes and reduce wear and tear on infrastructure. Additionally, investing in sustainable infrastructure, such as public transportation and renewable energy sources, can reduce the environmental footprint of tourism (Fahmi et al., 2023). Businesses within the tourism sector can also play a significant role in promoting sustainability. Hotels can adopt green practices, such as using energy-efficient lighting, reducing water consumption, and sourcing locally produced food. Tour operators can offer eco-friendly tours that emphasize conservation and educate travelers about the importance of protecting natural and cultural heritage. By highlighting their commitment to sustainability, businesses can attract environmentally conscious travelers and differentiate themselves in a competitive market.

Educating travelers about the importance of responsible travel behavior is key to achieving sustainable tourism. This involves raising awareness about the impact of their actions on the environment and local communities and encouraging them to make more sustainable choices. For instance, travelers can be encouraged to reduce their carbon footprint by opting for public transportation, cycling, or walking instead of using private cars. They can also be advised to respect local cultures and traditions, support local businesses, and minimize waste by using reusable items and avoiding single-use plastics (Ovezik et al., 2024). Destination authorities and tourism organizations can run awareness campaigns and provide information on sustainable practices through brochures, websites, and social media. Additionally, they can partner with influencers and travel bloggers to spread the message of sustainable tourism to a wider audience.

Achieving a balance between tourism growth and preservation of natural and cultural resources is essential for the long-term sustainability of the industry. This requires a holistic approach that considers the needs of all stakeholders, including tourists, local communities, businesses, and the environment. One effective strategy is the development of comprehensive tourism management plans that outline clear objectives and actions for sustainable tourism development. These plans should be based on thorough research and stakeholder consultations, ensuring that they address the specific challenges and opportunities of each destination. For example, a destination management plan for a coastal area might focus on protecting marine ecosystems, promoting eco-tourism activities, and supporting local fishermen and artisans (Fahmi et al., 2023). Collaboration between

42 *The Future of Blockchain in Tourism and Hospitality*

different stakeholders is also crucial for the successful implementation of sustainable tourism practices. However, it faces persistent challenges Governments, businesses, and local communities must work together to create policies and initiatives that promote sustainability and ensure that the benefits of tourism are distributed equitably. Public–private partnerships can be particularly effective in leveraging resources and expertise to address complex challenges.

Role of blockchain in enhancing transparency and trust in tourism industry

The tourism industry, a dynamic and multifaceted sector, is fundamental to the global economy. However, it faces persistent challenges related to transparency, trust, and operational efficiency. Blockchain technology, with its decentralized and immutable nature, offers a transformative solution to these issues. This chapter delves into how blockchain can enhance transparency and trust in the tourism industry by examining its potential applications in booking platforms, payment systems, and loyalty programs. It also addresses the challenges and considerations associated with adopting blockchain technology in this sector. Blockchain is a decentralized ledger technology that records transactions across multiple computers in a manner that ensures the security and immutability of the data. Each block in a blockchain contains a list of transactions, and these blocks are linked together in a chronological chain. This structure makes it nearly impossible to alter any information without altering all subsequent blocks, requiring the consensus of the majority of network participants (Treiblmaier and Önder, 2019).

1 **Decentralization:** No single entity controls the entire blockchain network. Control is distributed among all participants, enhancing the security and reliability of the network and making it less susceptible to fraud and manipulation (Erceg et al., 2020).
2 **Transparency:** All transactions recorded on the blockchain are visible to all participants, promoting accountability and trust. Once a transaction is recorded, it cannot be altered or deleted, ensuring the immutability of the data (Prados-Castillo et al., 2023).
3 **Security:** Blockchain employs advanced cryptographic techniques to secure data. Each block contains a unique cryptographic hash of the previous block, creating a secure link between them and

making it extremely difficult for hackers to alter any information (Ratna et al., 2024).

Transparency and trust are crucial in the tourism industry, where multiple stakeholders, including travelers, service providers, and intermediaries, interact and rely on accurate and reliable information. Blockchain technology addresses these core challenges by providing a decentralized, transparent, and secure platform for recording and verifying transactions. One of the primary applications of blockchain in tourism is in booking platforms. Traditional booking systems often involve multiple intermediaries, leading to increased costs and potential for fraud. Blockchain-powered booking platforms can eliminate these intermediaries, providing a secure and transparent environment for travelers to book accommodations, flights, and tours (Ozdemir et al., 2020). Fraudulent bookings and data tampering are significant issues in the tourism industry. Blockchain can address these problems through its transparent and immutable ledger. All booking transactions are recorded on the blockchain, making it easy to verify the authenticity of bookings and prevent fraud. Travelers and service providers can trust that the information on the blockchain is accurate and has not been tampered with (Zhang et al., 2023).

Blockchain technology enhances data privacy and control for travelers. Traditional booking systems often require travelers to share personal information with multiple intermediaries, increasing the risk of data breaches. Blockchain allows travelers to maintain control over their personal information, sharing it only with authorized parties through secure, encrypted transactions (Asif and Hassan, 2023).

Smart contracts are self-executing agreements with the terms of the contract directly written into code. These contracts automatically execute transactions when predefined conditions are met, ensuring secure and efficient transactions in the tourism industry (Ratna et al., 2024). Smart contracts can automate various aspects of the booking process, reducing the need for intermediaries and streamlining operations. For example, a smart contract can automatically confirm a booking and transfer payment to the service provider once the traveler completes the payment. This reduces the likelihood of disputes and ensures a smoother booking experience for travelers (Zhang et al., 2023). Traditional booking systems often involve high transaction fees due to the involvement of multiple intermediaries. Blockchain can significantly reduce these costs by enabling direct transactions between travelers and service providers. This not only makes travel more affordable for consumers but also increases profitability for service providers (Erceg et al., 2020).

Blockchain technology offers a revolutionary approach to payment systems in the tourism industry. Traditional payment methods can be slow, costly, and vulnerable to fraud. Blockchain-based payment systems, leveraging cryptocurrencies like Bitcoin and Ethereum, offer fast, secure, and cost-effective payment solutions (Lui et al., 2023). Blockchain enables secure and efficient payment transactions. Cryptocurrencies allow travelers to make direct payments to service providers without the need for intermediaries, reducing transaction times and costs. Additionally, blockchain's transparent and immutable ledger ensures accurate payment records, fostering trust among stakeholders (Handayani et al., 2023).

Tourists often face challenges related to currency exchange, including fluctuating exchange rates and high conversion fees. Cryptocurrencies provide a universal payment method, eliminating the need for currency exchange and reducing associated costs. This makes transactions more straightforward and cost-effective for travelers and service providers alike (Lui et al., 2023). Loyalty programs are a crucial aspect of customer engagement in the tourism industry. However, traditional loyalty programs often suffer from inefficiencies and lack of transparency. Blockchain technology can transform loyalty programs by providing transparent and interoperable solutions for travelers and businesses (Kirkwood, 2022). Blockchain-based loyalty programs enable seamless earning and redemption of rewards across various providers. Travelers can earn rewards from one service provider and redeem them with another, creating a more flexible and attractive loyalty ecosystem. This interoperability enhances customer engagement and promotes retention (Zhang et al., 2023). Blockchain ensures the security and integrity of loyalty programs. All transactions related to earning and redeeming rewards are recorded on the blockchain, preventing fraud and ensuring the accurate tracking of rewards. Travelers can manage their rewards confidently and securely, knowing that their information is protected (Kirkwood, 2022).

Emerging trends

Several emerging trends in blockchain technology are likely to shape the future of the tourism industry:

Blockchain in tourism: Opportunities and applications   45

1 **Integration with IoT:** Combining blockchain with the IoT can enhance data accuracy and security. For instance, IoT devices can automatically record and verify transactions on the blockchain, improving operational efficiency and trust (Prados-Castillo et al., 2023).

2 **AI and Blockchain Synergy:** Integrating AI with blockchain can optimize operations and personalize services. AI can analyze blockchain data to provide insights into traveler preferences and behavior, enabling more tailored and efficient service delivery (Treiblmaier and Önder, 2019).

3 **Sustainable Tourism:** Blockchain can support sustainable tourism by providing transparent and traceable records of environmental impact. Travelers can make informed choices based on verifiable data about the sustainability practices of service providers (Erceg et al., 2020).

Blockchain technology holds the promise of fundamentally transforming the tourism industry by enhancing transparency, trust, and operational efficiency. Its decentralized, transparent, and secure nature addresses core challenges faced by the industry, fostering a more reliable and efficient ecosystem. As blockchain technology continues to evolve and mature, its applications in tourism are expected to expand, driving the industry toward a more sustainable and resilient future. By adopting blockchain solutions, tourism businesses can unlock new opportunities for innovation and growth, ultimately benefiting travelers, service providers, and all stakeholders involved.

Case studies of successful tourism management

Iceland: Balancing tourism and environmental protection

Iceland is a prime example of a destination that has successfully managed the challenges of rapid tourism growth while protecting its natural environment. In recent years, Iceland has experienced a significant increase in tourist arrivals, driven by its stunning landscapes and unique cultural experiences. To manage this growth sustainably, the Icelandic government has implemented several measures. One key initiative is the establishment of the Icelandic Tourist Board, which oversees the development and implementation of sustainable tourism policies. The board works closely with local communities

46   *The Future of Blockchain in Tourism and Hospitality*

and businesses to promote responsible travel behavior and ensure that tourism benefits are distributed fairly. Additionally, Iceland has introduced a Nature Pass, a fee that tourists pay to access certain natural sites, with the revenue used to fund conservation efforts and maintain infrastructure (Nagel and Kranz, 2020). Furthermore, Iceland has invested in public transportation and green energy to reduce the environmental impact of tourism. The country aims to become carbon-neutral by 2040, and tourism plays a crucial role in achieving this goal by promoting eco-friendly travel options and reducing carbon emissions.

Bhutan: A model of high-value, low-impact tourism

Bhutan is renowned for its unique approach to tourism, which focuses on high-value, low-impact travel. The country restricts the number of tourists through a policy that requires visitors to book their trips through licensed tour operators and pay a daily fee that covers accommodation, meals, and a sustainable development fee. This policy ensures that tourism revenue is reinvested in the local economy and used to fund social and environmental initiatives. Bhutan's approach has helped preserve its cultural heritage and natural environment, while providing a high-quality experience for visitors. The country's commitment to sustainability is also reflected in its Gross National Happiness index, which prioritizes the well-being of its citizens and the protection of the environment over economic growth (Nagel and Kranz, 2020).

Innovation and technology have the potential to address many of the challenges facing the tourism industry. For instance, advancements in security technology can enhance the safety of travelers and build trust. Biometric identification systems, such as facial recognition, can streamline security checks at airports and border crossings, reducing wait times and improving the accuracy of identity verification. Additionally, mobile apps and online platforms can provide real-time updates on security conditions, travel advisories, and emergency contacts, helping travelers stay informed and safe (Hoffman et al., 2020). Technology also offers new opportunities for digital marketing and customer engagement. Social media platforms, travel blogs, and review sites have become essential tools for travelers seeking information and recommendations. Tourism businesses can leverage these platforms to connect with potential customers, showcase their offerings, and build a loyal following. Personalized marketing strategies, powered by data analytics, can target specific customer segments with tailored messages and offers, enhancing the overall travel experience (Any et al., 2024). VR and AR technologies are transforming the way people plan and experience travel. VR can provide immersive previews of destinations, allowing travelers to explore attractions and accommodations before making a booking. AR can enhance on-site experiences by overlaying digital information onto the physical environment, providing interactive guides and educational content. These technologies not only enrich the travel experience but also help manage visitor flow and reduce the impact on sensitive sites by offering virtual alternatives (Ovezik et al., 2024).

Case studies: Implementing blockchain in tourism sector around the world

Winding Tree is a decentralized travel marketplace that leverages blockchain technology to connect travelers directly with service providers. By eliminating intermediaries, Winding Tree reduces costs and increases transparency in the booking process. The platform uses smart contracts to automate transactions, ensuring secure and efficient bookings. Winding Tree's blockchain-based approach fosters trust and transparency, making it a promising solution for the tourism industry ((Dreyfuss, 2021).

TUI Group, one of the world's leading tourism companies, has embraced blockchain technology to enhance its operations. TUI uses blockchain to manage its inventory and streamline the distribution of travel services. By recording inventory data on the blockchain, TUI ensures the accuracy and transparency of its inventory records. This reduces the risk of overbooking and improves the efficiency of its operations. TUI's adoption of blockchain demonstrates the technology's potential to enhance transparency and trust in the tourism industry (TUI Group, 2016).

Webjet, an online travel agency, has implemented a blockchain-based solution to address the issue of hotel booking disputes. The platform uses blockchain to create a transparent and immutable record of booking transactions, reducing the likelihood of disputes and ensuring accurate payment records. Webjet's blockchain solution enhances trust among travelers and service providers,

48 The Future of Blockchain in Tourism and Hospitality

providing a more reliable and efficient booking experience (Webjetlimited, 20218.

The Alastria project in Spain is creating a digital ID system to simplify tourist operations by centralizing individual information. In 2018, Dubai launched Tourism 2.0, a blockchain marketplace connecting buyers directly with hotels and tour operators. True Tickets uses blockchain for secure ticketing, enhancing transparency and security (Fragnière, et al., 2021). Similarly, the UK's Digital Catapult center, funded by the government, supports early adoption of advanced digital technologies in industry.

TravelChain, a Russian project, is developing a unique database for tourists that securely encrypts personal data while keeping digital footprints publicly accessible. This decentralized registry allows businesses to analyze market needs and tailor personalized offers. Travel Token powers the ecosystem, enabling companies to obtain processed data from an AI service and facilitating data sharing among users and services through token transactions (Marco Valeri, 2020).

LockTrip is a comprehensive project that intersects travel with blockchain technology. Through its platform, users can purchase travel accommodations at competitive rates compared to major competitors like Booking.com and Airbnb. Utilizing blockchain, LockTrip features a decentralized booking engine called the LOC Ledger, integrated with a marketplace. Property owners and hoteliers can easily join the decentralized ecosystem. Additionally, LockTrip offers an exchange mechanism converting foreign currency into LOC at the time of booking. Notably, the platform is free for both hosts and guests, regardless of property numbers or revenue generated (Halkiopoulos et al., 2023).

The Smart Trip platform is designed as a decentralized ecosystem connecting travelers and service providers, offering comprehensive support for secure, convenient, and authentic travel experiences. It addresses common challenges travelers face, such as dealing with foreign currencies, language barriers, and finding suitable services. By enabling direct interaction among users, the platform streamlines trip planning, saves costs, and fosters a dynamic community. Smart Trip offers a wide range of services, from boat rentals to safaris, and serves as a valuable repository of travel knowledge. This innovative concept reduces research time and enhances the authenticity of travel experiences (Ozdemir et al., 2020).

Blockchain in tourism: Opportunities and applications 49

GOeureka (GOT) is a travel tech company using blockchain to create a hotel booking platform. Their recent platform alpha allows commission-free bookings with loyalty rewards. GOeureka pioneers blockchain-based bookings through Ethereum smart contracts, leveraging a vast hotel network. Its board includes executives from Accor Hotels and Agoda, bringing industry expertise. With access to over 400,000 hotels, GOeureka has a competitive edge. Unlike traditional booking sites charging high commissions, GOeureka offers transparent pricing and eliminates intermediaries, benefiting consumers and hotels alike by reducing costs and increasing efficiency (Halkiopoulos et al., 2023).

The Etherisc App is a platform dedicated to developing decentralized insurance solutions. With a focus on various sectors within the insurance industry, including airline delay insurance, Etherisc utilizes blockchain technology to address inefficiencies like high processing fees and lengthy claims processing times. The company has already introduced six innovative decentralized insurance applications, some of which extend their services to the tourism industry (Halkiopoulos et al., 2023).

The Beenest App operates as a decentralized network enabling cryptocurrency enthusiasts to share their homes, akin to Airbnb. Utilizing the Bee Token, users can book accommodations through the Beenest platform. Furthermore, in collaboration with WeTrust, the company plans to develop blockchain-based insurance specifically tailored for Beenest homeowners (Halkiopoulos et al., 2023).

The Caribbean island, several small island destinations in **the Caribbean,** which rely heavily on tourism, are investing in blockchain technology (BCT) platforms. These platforms are intended to directly connect tourists with local hotels and restaurants, thereby minimizing economic leakage and enhancing the socio-economic well-being of local communities (Kwok and Koh, 2019).

The tourism industry operates within a complex and evolving landscape shaped by emerging trends and persistent challenges. Security risks, trust issues, and sustainability concerns present significant hurdles that must be addressed to ensure the continued growth and success of the sector. By embracing innovation, advocating sustainability, and prioritizing trust and safety, the tourism industry can surmount these challenges and continue to thrive as a pivotal driver

50 *The Future of Blockchain in Tourism and Hospitality*

of global economic development and cultural interchange. Through collaborative efforts and a commitment to responsible practices, stakeholders can create a resilient and sustainable tourism sector that offers enduring and enriching experiences to travelers worldwide.

Thus, blockchain technology presents a wealth of opportunities and applications within the tourism industry, potentially enhancing transparency, building trust, and optimizing operational efficiency. By adopting blockchain-based solutions, tourism businesses can create safer, more seamless, and rewarding travel experiences, ultimately fostering growth and sustainability in the global tourism sector. With its capacity to transform various aspects of the tourism industry, blockchain technology is poised to play a pivotal role in shaping the future of travel experiences for businesses and the millions of tourists who embark on journeys each year.

3 Smart contracts and automation in the travel industry

Blockchain technology's significant innovation, smart contracts, presents ample advantages and opportunities for automating diverse processes within the tourism sector (Benduch, 2019). At the heart of blockchain technology are smart contracts, which represent self-executing agreements programmed to conduct transactions automatically upon meeting predetermined conditions. Unlike conventional contracts, smart contracts function autonomously within decentralized blockchain networks, removing intermediaries, streamlining processes, and ensuring agreements are executed autonomously and securely (Pradhan and Singh, 2021).

Figure 3.1 is a diagram that shows how blockchain technology is being used in different industries and the different application areas of this technology. With blockchain in a central position, this diagram highlights the many different industries and use cases that revolve around it. At the center of the diagram is the blockchain. This shows that blockchain underpins and enables innovation in all of these different use cases. Right around the blockchain are the main application areas. This represents the areas where blockchain technology is most widely used. The areas in this circle highlight blockchain's strengths and opportunities well.

1 **Cryptocurrency:** The most prominent application of blockchain technology, cryptocurrencies enable the secure and decentralized transfer of digital value. Cryptocurrencies such as Bitcoin and Ethereum are the most prominent examples in this area.

DOI: 10.4324/9781003521617-4

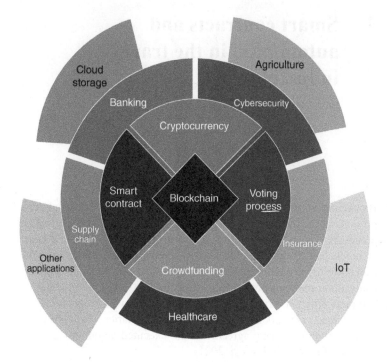

Figure 3.1 Blockchain applications.

Source: Rajasekaran et al. (2022).

2 **Smart contracts:** These are programmed agreements that are automatically executed when certain conditions are met. The Ethereum blockchain pioneered the popularization of this type of contract.
3 **Crowdfunding:** Blockchain provides decentralized and transparent fundraising mechanisms. In particular, ICOs (initial coin offerings) are used to provide initial funding for projects.
4 **Voting process:** Blockchain can increase transparency and security in voting processes. Digital voting systems can reduce the risk of fraud and enable quick verification of results.

The outer circle shows other broad application areas for blockchain technology. These areas show how blockchain can be integrated into different industries and transform the way they operate:

Smart contracts and automation in travel industry 53

1 **Agriculture:** Blockchain is being used to track the supply chain of agricultural products and promote sustainable agricultural practices. The journey of products from farm to fork becomes more transparent.
2 **Cybersecurity:** Blockchain offers new approaches to secure data and protect against cyberattacks. Decentralization can protect data integrity and confidentiality.
3 **Insurance:** In the insurance sector, smart contracts can enable the automated execution of policies and the rapid processing of claims. This makes processes more efficient and transparent.
4 **Internet of Things (IoT):** Blockchain enables IoT devices to securely communicate with each other. This increases data sharing and transaction accuracy.
5 **Healthcare:** Blockchain allows patient data to be stored in a secure and immutable manner. It can also facilitate data sharing among healthcare providers.
6 **Supply chain:** Blockchain is used to track and verify the journey of products through the supply chain. This reduces the risk of counterfeiting and ensures the authenticity of products.
7 **Banking:** Blockchain can speed up cross-border transactions and authentication processes in the banking sector and reduce costs.
8 **Cloud storage:** Blockchain enables decentralized data storage. This increases data security and reduces storage costs.
9 **Other applications:** Blockchain has the potential to provide innovative solutions in many other areas. It can be used in many sectors, from education to entertainment, from energy management to legal services.

This diagram clearly shows how blockchain technology has a wide range of applications and how it is becoming a transformative force in many sectors. The centrality of blockchain highlights how it underpins all of these areas and drives innovation. As the technology evolves, blockchain is expected to be used in more and more areas.

Smart contracts offer manifold benefits like operational efficiency and cost reduction by eliminating intermediaries and automating tasks (Negi, 2021). These digital contracts promise to optimize various tourism operations, including accommodation bookings, payment processing, and loyalty program management. Consequently, workflow efficiency improves, administrative burdens decrease, and resource utilization is enhanced, resulting in expedited transactions,

54　*The Future of Blockchain in Tourism and Hospitality*

seamless bookings, and enhanced cost efficiency for enterprises and travelers.

Operating on decentralized blockchain networks, smart contracts offer unparalleled transparency and trustworthiness. Transactions recorded on the blockchain are immutable and transparent, providing a verifiable activity record (Karinsalo and Halunen, 2018). This transparency nurtures trust among stakeholders, ensuring agreements execute as intended and maintaining data integrity throughout. Smart contracts provide a secure and transparent framework for conducting business transactions, validating transaction authenticity, ensuring contractual compliance, or verifying identity (Prados-Castillo et al., 2023). Furthermore, smart contracts aim to minimize human error risk and ensure accurate, reliable transaction execution. Automating routine tasks and enforcing predefined rules enhance operational efficiency, reduce errors, and boost reliability (Treiblmaier and Önder, 2019). These digital contracts manage various tasks such as payment calculations, reservation updates, or loyalty reward management, executing agreements automatically based on preset conditions (Ozdemir et al., 2020).

Integrating smart contracts into various tourism processes enables automation and efficiency enhancements throughout the travel lifecycle (Ovezik et al., 2024). For instance, in booking and reservation processes, smart contracts streamline agreement execution based on conditions like availability, pricing, and payment confirmation. This enables travelers to seamlessly book accommodations, transportation, and activities, with the smart contract overseeing the entire process from initiation to confirmation (Vasani et al., 2024). Regarding payment processes, smart contracts facilitate secure, transparent transactions between travelers and service providers, automating transactions and enforcing predefined rules. By automating payment processes and reducing intermediaries, they minimize error, delay, and dispute risks, ensuring seamless, transparent transaction execution (Xu and Sun, 2024).

Smart contracts can revolutionize loyalty programs by automating reward accrual and redemption based on predefined criteria (Xu and Sun, 2024). With smart contracts managing reward distribution and redemption across participating providers, travelers can earn rewards seamlessly for their transactions. Smart contracts ensure accurate, transparent reward calculation by automating reward processes and fostering customer engagement and loyalty (Treiblmaier and Önder, 2019).

Technical insights into smart contracts

The travel sector, a cornerstone of global commerce and human interaction, is constantly seeking innovative solutions to streamline operations, enhance efficiency, and foster trust among stakeholders. In recent years, the advent of blockchain technology has sparked significant interest and exploration within the travel industry. One of the most promising applications of blockchain technology in travel is the utilization of smart contracts, which redefine how agreements are conducted and managed. This chapter aims to provide a comprehensive exploration of smart contracts in the travel industry, elucidating their technical insights, advantages, and potential impacts on various facets of the sector. Smart contracts represent a groundbreaking utilization of blockchain technology, revolutionizing the way agreements are executed and enforced. At its core, a smart contract is a self-executing agreement encoded directly into computer code. These contracts are designed to automatically enforce and execute terms when pre-established conditions are met, without the need for intermediaries (Spychiger et al., 2021).

By operating within blockchain networks, smart contracts offer enhanced transparency, security, and immutability. Blockchain networks, the underlying infrastructure for smart contracts, can generally be classified into four main types: public, private, consortium, and hybrid. Public blockchains, exemplified by Bitcoin, Ethereum, and Litecoin, have no restrictions on access, allowing anyone online to join as a node. Transactions within public blockchains are anonymous yet transparent. Private blockchains, on the other hand, have restricted access controlled by a single entity. These networks operate on a closed network, making them suitable for internal company applications. Consortium blockchains bridge public and private networks, jointly managed by multiple coordinating organizations, allowing for a blend of public and private data. Hybrid blockchains combine features of both private and public systems, with records not publicly viewable by default but verifiable when needed through mechanisms like smart contracts (Zwitter and Hazenberg, 2020).

Consensus algorithms, crucial for maintaining the integrity and security of blockchain networks, can be categorized into proof-based and vote-based systems. Proof-based systems, prevalent in public blockchains, require members to prove satisfying a task for rewards. In contrast, vote-based approaches, typical of private or consortium

56　*The Future of Blockchain in Tourism and Hospitality*

chains, involve members voting with majority acceptance. The choice of consensus algorithm often depends on the specific requirements and characteristics of the blockchain network (Saulina and Delhi, 2024).

The integration of smart contracts in the travel sector holds immense potential for transforming traditional processes and enhancing efficiency. By removing intermediaries, smart contracts promote direct peer-to-peer interaction, streamlining the booking process and reducing transaction costs. This streamlined approach benefits both businesses and travelers, leading to increased satisfaction and long-term loyalty (Hoffman et al., 2020).

Automation is a central tenet of smart contracts, enabling the seamless execution of agreements without manual intervention. By encoding contractual terms into code, smart contracts automatically enforce predefined conditions, minimizing the risk of errors, disputes, and misunderstandings. The transparent and tamper-proof nature of smart contracts significantly enhances trust between parties, as every transaction executed through these contracts is recorded on the blockchain, ensuring transparency and immutability (Treiblmaier and Önder, 2019). Furthermore, the decentralized and transparent ledger enabled by smart contracts allows stakeholders to verify the authenticity of transactions, fostering trust and confidence in the system. Smart contracts optimize workflows and reduce administrative overhead within the travel industry by automating routine tasks, eliminating unnecessary intermediaries, and ensuring accurate and reliable execution of agreements (Erceg et al., 2020).

Removing intermediaries facilitated by smart contracts promotes direct peer-to-peer interaction, enhancing efficiency and transparency in the booking process. This streamlined approach benefits businesses and travelers, increasing satisfaction and long-term loyalty (Hoffman et al., 2020). Automation lies at the heart of smart contracts, enabling seamless execution of agreements without manual intervention. By encoding contractual terms into code, smart contracts automatically enforce predefined conditions, minimizing the risk of errors, disputes, and misunderstandings (Saulina and Delhi, 2024).

The transparent and tamper-proof nature of smart contracts significantly enhances trust between parties, as every transaction executed through these contracts is recorded on the blockchain, ensuring transparency and immutability (Treiblmaier and Önder, 2019). The decentralized and transparent ledger enables stakeholders to verify the authenticity of transactions, fostering trust and confidence in the system

(Erceg et al., 2020). Smart contracts optimize workflows and reduce administrative overhead within the travel industry. By automating routine tasks, eliminating unnecessary intermediaries, and ensuring accurate and reliable execution of agreements, smart contracts contribute to faster transactions, reduced costs, and improved customer satisfaction (Benduch, 2019).

The versatility of smart contracts extends to various aspects of the travel industry, offering solutions for booking platforms, payment systems, and loyalty programs, among others. Smart contracts automate reservation processes, facilitate secure and transparent payments, and streamline loyalty management, driving growth and innovation in the global tourism sector (Pradhan and Singh, 2021). The adoption of smart contracts powered by blockchain technology is poised to reshape traditional operations and introduce a more transparent, efficient, and customer-centric experience within the travel industry. Smart contracts are expected to enhance efficiency and trust across the travel lifecycle as technology evolves, paving the way for a brighter future in the global tourism sector.

The adoption of smart contracts powered by blockchain technology is poised to reshape traditional operations and introduce a more transparent, efficient, and customer-centric experience within the travel industry. By removing intermediaries and automating processes, smart contracts reduce costs, increase efficiency, and enhance trust between stakeholders. This, in turn, leads to improved customer satisfaction, increased loyalty, and sustainable growth in the global tourism sector. Moreover, smart contracts have the potential to drive innovation and collaboration within the travel industry, fostering new business models and partnerships. As technology evolves and blockchain adoption increases, smart contracts will continue to play a crucial role in optimizing workflows, reducing administrative overhead, and enhancing transparency across the travel lifecycle. In conclusion, smart contracts represent a transformative innovation within the travel industry, leveraging blockchain technology to redefine how agreements are conducted and managed. By automating processes, removing intermediaries, and enhancing transparency, smart contracts offer significant benefits for businesses, travelers, and other stakeholders. The adoption of smart contracts is expected to reshape traditional operations and introduce a more efficient, transparent, and customer-centric experience within the travel sector. As technology continues to evolve, smart contracts will continue to play a pivotal

58 *The Future of Blockchain in Tourism and Hospitality*

role in driving innovation, collaboration, and growth in the global tourism industry.

Regulatory and legal considerations for smart contracts in tourism

Smart contracts serve as the backbone of automation in the tourism industry, providing streamlined and innovative solutions that significantly enhance operational efficiency and elevate the overall travel experience for customers (Ratna et al., 2024). Smart contracts have emerged as a transformative force in the tourism industry, offering streamlined and innovative solutions that significantly enhance operational efficiency and elevate the overall travel experience for customers (Ratna et al., 2024). Leveraging blockchain technology, smart contracts automate agreements between travelers and service providers, facilitating seamless and hassle-free booking processes based on predefined conditions. However, as smart contracts continue to gain traction in the tourism sector, it becomes imperative to examine the regulatory and legal considerations surrounding their implementation. This paper provides a detailed exploration of the regulatory frameworks, legal challenges, and emerging trends shaping the adoption of smart contracts in tourism, offering insights into their implications for stakeholders. As smart contracts become increasingly integrated into the tourism industry, regulators around the world are grappling with the need to adapt existing legal frameworks to accommodate this innovative technology. While smart contracts offer numerous benefits, including efficiency, transparency, and security, they also present unique regulatory challenges, particularly in areas such as contract law, consumer protection, and data privacy.

Smart contracts operate within the framework of traditional contract law, wherein agreements are formed based on mutual consent, offer, acceptance, and consideration. However, the automated nature of smart contracts raises questions about the enforceability of contractual terms and the role of intermediaries in resolving disputes. Regulators must clarify the legal status of smart contracts and establish guidelines for their formation, execution, and enforcement to ensure compliance with existing contract law principles. Consumer protection is another critical consideration in the adoption of smart contracts in tourism. While these contracts offer convenience and efficiency for travelers, they also entail risks, such as potential vulnerabilities in code, lack

Smart contracts and automation in travel industry 59

of recourse in case of errors, and limited legal remedies for disputes. Regulators must enact measures to safeguard consumer interests, including disclosure requirements, dispute resolution mechanisms, and liability frameworks, to mitigate these risks and ensure fair and transparent transactions. Data privacy is a paramount concern in the era of smart contracts, as these contracts rely on blockchain technology to store and transmit sensitive information securely. However, the decentralized nature of blockchain poses challenges to traditional data protection laws, such as the EU's General Data Protection Regulation (GDPR), which emphasize centralized control and accountability. Regulators must reconcile the tension between blockchain technology and data privacy laws by implementing privacy-preserving solutions, such as zero-knowledge proofs and multi-party computation, to enable secure and compliant smart contract transactions.

Despite the potential benefits of smart contracts, their implementation in the tourism industry is not without legal challenges. These challenges stem from various factors, including regulatory uncertainty, technological complexity, and contractual ambiguities, which may hinder widespread adoption and integration. One of the primary challenges facing smart contract implementation is regulatory uncertainty, as the legal status and treatment of these contracts vary across jurisdictions. While some countries have embraced blockchain technology and enacted supportive regulations, others remain skeptical or have yet to address the legal implications of smart contracts. This regulatory fragmentation complicates cross-border transactions and raises compliance concerns for businesses operating in multiple jurisdictions. Smart contracts are inherently complex, requiring expertise in both legal and technical domains to design, implement, and maintain effectively.

Legal professionals may lack the requisite knowledge and skills to navigate the intricacies of blockchain technology, while technical experts may struggle to understand the legal implications of smart contract code. Bridging this gap requires interdisciplinary collaboration and education to ensure that smart contracts comply with legal requirements and industry standards. Smart contracts introduce novel legal concepts and challenges that may not be adequately addressed by existing legal frameworks. For example, the immutable and self-executing nature of smart contracts raises questions about contractual interpretation, modification, and termination. Additionally, the use of oracles to retrieve external data for smart contract execution

60 *The Future of Blockchain in Tourism and Hospitality*

introduces potential points of failure and manipulation. Resolving these contractual ambiguities requires innovative legal solutions, such as smart contract templates, standardized terms, and dispute resolution mechanisms, to enhance clarity, predictability, and enforceability.

Despite the regulatory and legal challenges facing smart contracts, there are several emerging trends and developments that may shape their future adoption and regulation in the tourism industry. Given the global nature of tourism and blockchain technology, international collaboration is essential to harmonize regulatory frameworks, promote interoperability, and facilitate cross-border transactions (Saulina and Delhi, 2024). Organizations such as the International Organization for Standardization (ISO) and the International Chamber of Commerce (ICC) play a crucial role in developing industry standards and best practices for smart contracts, fostering trust and confidence among stakeholders. Regulatory sandboxes provide a controlled environment for testing and experimenting with innovative technologies, such as smart contracts, under regulatory supervision (Sankar and David, 2024).

By granting exemptions or waivers from certain legal requirements, regulators can encourage experimentation, foster innovation, and gather valuable insights into the potential risks and benefits of smart contracts in real-world scenarios. Countries such as Singapore, the United Kingdom, and Switzerland have implemented regulatory sandboxes to support blockchain-based initiatives in various sectors, including tourism. Self-regulatory initiatives, led by industry consortia, trade associations, and professional bodies, offer another avenue for addressing the regulatory challenges of smart contracts (Nagel and Kranz, 2020). These initiatives aim to establish industry standards, best practices, and codes of conduct for smart contract development, deployment, and governance. By promoting transparency, accountability, and ethical behavior, self-regulatory frameworks can enhance consumer trust, reduce regulatory burden, and foster responsible innovation in the tourism industry.

Smart contracts hold immense promise for transforming the tourism industry, offering streamlined processes, enhanced efficiency, and improved trust between travelers and service providers. However, their adoption is contingent upon addressing the regulatory and legal considerations surrounding their implementation. By developing clear and coherent regulatory frameworks, resolving legal challenges, and embracing emerging trends, policymakers, businesses, and

Smart contracts and automation in travel industry 61

other stakeholders can unlock the full potential of smart contracts in tourism, paving the way for a more seamless, secure, and rewarding travel experience for all.

Case study: Smart contract integration in Turkish and Italian hotel booking systems

A notable example of smart contracts being effectively integrated into the tourism industry is the strategic partnership between Turkish and Italian hotel booking systems, where these organizations have utilized smart contracts to automate and enhance the booking process, resulting in improved efficiency and customer satisfaction. By incorporating smart contracts into their respective hotel booking systems, Turkish and Italian hotel operators can provide travelers with a seamless, transparent, and secure booking experience. These digital agreements automatically execute and verify key booking aspects, such as availability, reservation confirmation, and payment processing, in real time. This level of automation substantially reduces the risk of errors, discrepancies, or delays, offering travelers accurate and timely booking confirmations, ultimately enhancing trust and overall customer satisfaction.

Smart contracts also offer Turkish and Italian hotel operators the opportunity to introduce unique and innovative loyalty programs, automating the accrual and redemption of customer rewards. This streamlined process enables travelers to earn and redeem rewards across multiple hotels and destinations, fostering customer loyalty and encouraging repeat business.

Interoperability, a core feature of smart contracts, makes it easy for travelers to manage rewards across multiple providers, enhancing customer engagement and loyalty. As a result, customers benefit from a more seamless, transparent, and rewarding travel experience, driving growth and innovation in the global tourism sector.

In conclusion, smart contracts offer significant benefits and opportunities for automating various processes within the tourism industry, including booking systems, payment processes, and loyalty programs. By leveraging blockchain-based smart contracts, travel businesses can streamline operations, reduce costs, and enhance customer satisfaction, leading to a more efficient and transparent travel experience for travelers and, ultimately, fostering a more sustainable and innovative tourism sector.

62 *The Future of Blockchain in Tourism and Hospitality*

Security challenges in implementing smart contracts

Smart contracts, a hallmark innovation brought forth by blockchain technology, have been lauded for their potential to revolutionize various industries, including finance, supply chain management, and healthcare. However, their implementation is not without challenges, particularly concerning security. In this comprehensive exploration, we delve into the intricate landscape of security challenges associated with smart contracts and propose strategies to mitigate these risks. Drawing insights from a plethora of scholarly articles and research papers, we aim to provide a holistic understanding of the security implications inherent in smart contract implementation. Smart contracts, self-executing agreements with the terms of the contract directly written into code, have gained considerable traction in recent years due to their potential to automate processes, eliminate intermediaries, and enhance transparency. These digital contracts, residing on a blockchain network, execute automatically when predetermined conditions are met, thereby streamlining transactions and reducing the risk of fraud.

Before delving into the security challenges, it is imperative to grasp the fundamentals of smart contracts. Initially proposed by Nick Szabo in the 1990s, smart contracts have evolved significantly with the advent of blockchain technology, particularly with the emergence of Ethereum, which introduced Turing-complete smart contracts capable of executing arbitrary code. Smart contracts are composed of code stored on a blockchain and are immutable, transparent, and decentralized, ensuring trust and efficiency in transactions. While smart contracts offer numerous advantages, their implementation poses several security challenges, ranging from vulnerabilities in the code to external threats targeting the underlying blockchain network. These challenges can be categorized into technical vulnerabilities, human errors, and regulatory compliance issues.

One of the primary security challenges associated with smart contracts is the presence of technical vulnerabilities in the code. Ovezik et al. (2024) highlight the susceptibility of smart contracts to various types of attacks, including reentrancy attacks, integer overflow/underflow, and denial-of-service attacks. These vulnerabilities stem from coding errors, such as improper input validation, inadequate testing, and unchecked external calls, which can be exploited by malicious actors to manipulate the contract's behavior and siphon funds.

Smart contracts and automation in travel industry 63

In addition to technical vulnerabilities, human errors pose a significant threat to the security of smart contracts. Developers may inadvertently introduce bugs or vulnerabilities into the code, leading to unforeseen consequences. Furthermore, the lack of standardized development practices and the absence of formal verification tools contribute to the proliferation of vulnerabilities in smart contracts. Erceg et al. (2020) discuss the complexity of smart contract development coupled with the rapid pace of innovation, which exacerbates the likelihood of human errors, making robust security protocols indispensable. Another critical aspect of smart contract security pertains to regulatory compliance. As smart contracts operate autonomously on a blockchain network, ensuring compliance with existing legal frameworks presents a formidable challenge. Regulatory uncertainty surrounding blockchain technology, coupled with the global nature of decentralized networks, complicates efforts to establish clear guidelines for smart contract implementation. Özgit and Adalıer (2022) emphasize that the immutable nature of blockchain transactions raises concerns regarding data privacy, consumer protection, and jurisdictional issues, necessitating a nuanced approach to regulatory compliance.

To address the security challenges associated with smart contracts, proactive measures must be implemented at various stages of the development lifecycle. These mitigation strategies encompass code auditing, formal verification, secure coding practices, and regulatory compliance frameworks. Conducting comprehensive code audits is paramount to identifying and rectifying vulnerabilities in smart contracts. Independent auditors with expertise in blockchain development meticulously review the codebase to uncover potential weaknesses and assess the contract's adherence to best practices. Furthermore, automated tools, such as static analysis and dynamic analysis, can augment the auditing process by detecting common coding errors and security flaws. Formal verification techniques, such as mathematical proofs and model checking, offer a rigorous approach to validating the correctness of smart contracts. Tyan et al. (2021) discuss how, by formally specifying the contract's properties and verifying its compliance with predefined requirements, developers can mitigate the risk of logical errors and ensure the contract behaves as intended under all possible scenarios. While formal verification imposes a higher upfront cost and requires specialized expertise, its benefits in terms of robustness and security are invaluable.

64   *The Future of Blockchain in Tourism and Hospitality*

Adhering to secure coding practices is essential to minimizing vulnerabilities in smart contracts. Developers should follow established guidelines, such as those outlined by the Open Zeppelin framework, to mitigate common security risks, including input validation, access control, and exception handling. By adopting a defensive programming mindset and incorporating security mechanisms into the codebase, developers can bolster the resilience of smart contracts against malicious attacks and unintended exploits. In navigating the complex regulatory landscape surrounding smart contracts, organizations must proactively engage with regulators and legal experts to ensure compliance with applicable laws and regulations.

Treiblmaier and Önder (2019) emphasize developing robust compliance frameworks that encompass data protection, consumer rights, and jurisdictional requirements is imperative to fostering trust and mitigating legal risks. Furthermore, embracing transparency and accountability in smart contract deployment facilitates regulatory oversight and enhances stakeholder confidence in the integrity of blockchain-based transactions. In conclusion, while smart contracts hold immense promise for revolutionizing various industries, their implementation is fraught with security challenges that necessitate careful consideration and proactive mitigation strategies. By addressing technical vulnerabilities, human errors, and regulatory compliance issues, organizations can harness the full potential of smart contracts while safeguarding against potential threats. As blockchain technology continues to evolve, fostering collaboration between industry stakeholders, academia, and policymakers is essential to fostering a secure and resilient ecosystem for smart contract innovation.

4 Blockchain's role in promoting sustainable tourism practices

The tourism sector is an important part of the world economy. However, the growth of this sector has also brought environmental and social problems. Sustainable tourism is a concept that has emerged to overcome these problems and reduce the negative impacts of tourism. Sustainable tourism is based on the principles of environmental, economic, and social sustainability (Hoffman et al., 2020). In this context, blockchain technology is an important tool to support sustainable tourism. Blockchain technology, with its capacity to provide secure, transparent, and immutable data records, can be applied in many areas of sustainable tourism. On the one hand, the tourism industry generates income and employment for local economies, but on the other hand, it can have negative impacts, such as overconsumption of natural resources, environmental pollution, and degradation of local cultures. Achieving this balance – making tourism sustainable – is an important part of the United Nations' 2030 Sustainable Development Goals (SDGs). However, current practices often fall short of achieving this balance, and the tourism sector as a whole tends to move away from sustainability (Edastama et al., 2021).

Technological advances offer great potential to support sustainable tourism. In this context, blockchain technology, which has attracted a great deal of attention in recent years, has the potential to revolutionize various sectors, and the tourism sector can benefit from the opportunities offered by this technology (Lui et al., 2023). The basis of blockchain technology is the storage and management of data in a decentralized network. This technology ensures that data is stored in a secure and unalterable way. This feature of blockchain has great potential in sustainable tourism applications. For example, managing

DOI: 10.4324/9781003521617-5

66   *The Future of Blockchain in Tourism and Hospitality*

transactions in the tourism sector in a transparent and secure way offers many advantages, such as preventing fraud and reducing costs (Asif and Hassan, 2023).

Understanding what sustainable tourism is and what challenges it faces is important to assess the potential impact of blockchain technology in this field. Sustainable tourism aims to create opportunities for both current and future generations, taking into account the economic, social, and environmental impacts of tourism. This includes the effort to conserve natural resources and preserve local cultural values while improving the well-being of local people. Blockchain technology provides many advantages in achieving sustainable tourism goals. These advantages include making transactions secure and transparent, preventing fraud, reducing costs, and supporting local economies. These potential contributions of blockchain are manifested in various application areas in the tourism sector (Nagel and Kranz, 2020).

Blockchain technology's contribution to sustainable tourism

Reservation Systems: Travel reservations can be made more secure and efficient with blockchain technology. For example, smart contracts can be used for hotel reservations, airline tickets, and other travel services. These contracts are automatically executed when certain conditions are met and prevent fraud. Blockchain-based reservation systems reduce costs by eliminating intermediaries and enable transactions to be carried out faster and more securely (Name and Choi, 2022).

Tourism Information Management: Blockchain makes tourism information management more transparent. By providing reliable and verifiable information about tourism destinations and service providers, it enables tourists to make informed decisions. For example, a hotel's sustainability practices can be verified and transparently presented on the blockchain. This allows tourists to choose eco-friendly hotels and restaurants (Willie, 2019).

Loyalty Programs: Loyalty programs in the tourism industry can be managed through blockchain-based digital wallets. Tourists can store the points they earn during their travels in blockchain-based digital wallets and redeem these points for hotel stays, airline tickets, or other tourism services. This system ensures secure and transparent management of points and prevents fraud (Dogru et al., 2018).

Environmental Impact Monitoring: Blockchain technology can also be used for sustainability and environmental impact monitoring in the tourism sector. Tourism businesses can monitor and report their environmental impact on blockchain. This allows tourists and other stakeholders to see their sustainability practices transparently. For example, a hotel can track and report environmental data, such as energy consumption, water usage, and waste management, on the blockchain. This data plays an important role in achieving sustainability goals (Goudarzi and Martin, 2018).

Safe Travel and Health Information: The COVID-19 pandemic has increased the importance of health and safety in the tourism industry. Blockchain technology can be used to securely manage tourists' health information. For example, tourists' vaccination records or COVID-19 test results can be securely stored on the blockchain and verified to the relevant authorities. This ensures that tourists have a safe and healthy travel experience (Irvin and Sullivan, 2018).

Intermediaries in tourism operations can increase costs and reduce the economic benefits for both tourists and local service providers. Blockchain technology makes it possible to carry out transactions without intermediaries by enabling a secure and transparent exchange of information (Pilkington, 2017). This enables small local businesses and tourism service providers to interact directly with tourists, supporting the local economy and culture. For example, the ability of locals to sell products and services directly to tourists gives tourists access to authentic travel experiences. Opportunities such as tourists being able to stay in a local home instead of a hotel and receive recommendations on local restaurants or sacred sites will benefit both tourists and locals. Furthermore, by using blockchain-based digital currencies, local communities can create their own money, and tourists can use it to contribute to the local economy (Tham and Sigala, 2020).

From an environmental sustainability perspective, blockchain technology can positively impact food supply chain management and food logistics management. Through the transparency, reliability, and immutability of data, blockchain technology guarantees traceability systems, providing information on the origin, processing, and retailing of food products (Irvin and Sullivan, 2018). This system can ensure food safety, verify whether "green" food is really "green," limit the possibility of counterfeiting or fraud, and increase tourist confidence. Furthermore, food waste, a major problem in the tourism sector, can be reduced through effective inventory management, redistribution

68 *The Future of Blockchain in Tourism and Hospitality*

of excess food, recycling, and waste disposal. The decentralized, integrated nature of blockchain technology can improve inventory management and facilitate the distribution of excess food (Bell and Hollander, 2018).

Tourist satisfaction is one of the most important goals of sustainable tourism development. Tourism and hospitality companies place great emphasis on customer management, tourist experience, and service excellence to meet tourists' needs and expectations (Name and Choi, 2022). The application of blockchain technology to tourist services can significantly improve tourist satisfaction through services, such as tracking tourists, tracking their luggage, and facilitating travel insurance in case of flight delay or cancellation. Furthermore, blockchain technology can enable the customization of services without violating tourists' privacy. Through the use of digital identity, tourists can choose what data they want to share and with whom. Overall, blockchain technology can greatly contribute to the tourism sector by providing more accurate and reliable information, offering customized services, and enabling better tourist experiences and satisfaction (Ludeiro, 2019).

Increasing global awareness of sustainable tourism issues and increasing the willingness of individuals to contribute to sustainable tourism development is vital for the transition to a sustainable future. Blockchain technology can play an important role by providing transparent information about emissions, criteria, food supply chains, and tourists' preferences. Real and audible information on the blockchain can raise awareness and create incentives for sustainable behavior by all interested parties (Caddeo and Pinna, 2021).

Some tourists are predisposed to environmentally conscious behavior and show great interest in sustainable tourism practices, but others may not care about the impact of their behavior on the local community and the destination's environment. A blockchain-based reward system can help in changing tourists' behavior (Bell and Hollander, 2018). If tourists collect rewards for their sustainable behavior, for example, actions such as cleaning beaches or collecting plastic from the sea and taking it to recycling centers could become more likely. Also, tourists are more likely to opt for environmentally friendly hiking routes if they earn cryptocurrencies or tokens for their green behavior. Incentives are known to have a positive impact on the sustainable behavior of individuals. Blockchain technology can offer an excellent opportunity to incentivize the sustainable behavior of tourists. Tourists can earn tokens that they can spend to buy other goods and services in the host destination (Goudarzi and Martin, 2018).

Tourists with environmentally conscious behaviors often research reviews and ratings when choosing an accommodation or restaurant. However, the main problem may be the impossibility of knowing which reviews are genuine and reliable and which are not. Hotel and restaurant owners or customers can manipulate rating and review systems (Awerika et al., 2023. Blockchain technology can address this problem by creating a unique private key for each identity and embedding several independent verification processes in rating and review systems. This can reduce the rates of manipulation or duplication of reviews. Blockchain technology could be applied to create a voting system that could be used to create an immutable rating of the best accommodations and restaurants with sustainable tourism practices (Edastama et al., 2021).

The future of blockchain technology in sustainable tourism

Blockchain technology will play an important role in the future of sustainable tourism. This technology enables the tourism sector to be more efficient, fair, and sustainable (Huseynov and Mitchell, 2024). In the future, blockchain technology is expected to be more widely used in the tourism sector.

Smart Cities and Tourism: In the future, smart cities can support sustainable tourism practices using blockchain technology. By using blockchain technology for energy management, transportation, waste management, and other services, smart cities enable tourists to have more sustainable travel experiences. For example, smart cities can monitor and reduce tourists' carbon footprints, promote environmentally friendly transportation options, and support sustainable tourism practices (Any et al., 2024).

Sustainable Tourism Policies: In the future, sustainable tourism policies and regulations can be supported by blockchain technology. Using blockchain-based systems, governments and policymakers can monitor and evaluate the sustainability practices of tourism businesses. This plays an important role in achieving sustainable tourism goals and makes the tourism sector more transparent and accountable (Lutfiani et al., 2022).

Global Collaborations: Blockchain technology enables the creation of global collaborations and networks. Using blockchain-based

70 *The Future of Blockchain in Tourism and Hospitality*

systems, stakeholders in the tourism sector can share information and resources more efficiently and support sustainable tourism practices. This makes the tourism sector more resilient and sustainable and plays an important role in achieving global sustainability goals (Goudarzi and Martin, 2018).

Education and Awareness: In the future, blockchain technology can also be used for sustainable tourism education and awareness-raising. Through blockchain-based systems, tourism businesses and tourists can learn about and adopt sustainable tourism practices. This contributes to increased awareness of sustainability in the tourism sector and the spread of sustainable tourism practices (Treiblmaier and Önder, 2019).

Blockchain technology will play an important role in the future of sustainable tourism. This technology enables the tourism sector to be more efficient, fair, and sustainable. The opportunities offered by blockchain make tourism operations more transparent, secure, and sustainable (Fahmi et al., 2023). Therefore, it is important that tourism sector actors understand the opportunities offered by blockchain technology and integrate it into sustainable tourism development. This will not only help achieve current sustainability goals but also make the future of tourism more equitable, transparent, and resilient (Zwitter and Hazenberg, 2020). As a result, academics, policymakers, and industry leaders should delve deeper into the implications of blockchain technology on sustainable tourism and collaborate to better understand the potential of this technology. Understanding how blockchain technology can shape the tourism industry in the future and contribute to SDGs is critical to building a sustainable tourism future (Handayani et al., 2023). In this context, exploring how blockchain technology can transform sustainable tourism and how the tourism industry can achieve a more sustainable, fair, and transparent future is vital for the success of sustainable tourism.

Blockchain and the economic dimensions of sustainable tourism

Blockchain technology also offers significant opportunities to support economic sustainability in the tourism sector. Economic sustainability requires tourism activities to be financially viable and profitable in the long term (Nagel and Kranz, 2020). In this context, blockchain technology provides many economic advantages, such as reducing costs, preventing fraud, and creating new revenue models. Blockchain-based payment systems can help reduce costs in the tourism sector. Traditional payment systems can be costly, often with high transaction fees and long processing times. However, blockchain-based payment systems offer low transaction fees and fast processing times. This reduces costs for tourism businesses and allows them to offer more competitive prices (Asif and Hassan, 2023). Furthermore, blockchain-based payment systems further reduce costs by eliminating intermediaries and enabling transactions to be carried out more efficiently. Fraud prevention provides a significant economic advantage in the tourism sector. Fraud can lead to huge financial losses in the tourism industry and undermine confidence in the sector. Blockchain technology enables transactions to be recorded in a secure and unalterable way, which helps prevent fraud (Lui et al., 2023). For example, blockchain-based booking systems can help prevent fake bookings and fraud attempts. This reduces financial losses for tourism businesses and increases trust in the industry.

Blockchain technology also enables the creation of new revenue models in the tourism sector (Edastama et al., 2021). For example, blockchain-based tokenization can help tourism businesses create new sources of financing. Tokenization allows physical assets or services to be represented as digital tokens. These tokens can be purchased and traded by investors. For example, by tokenizing its property, a hotel can raise funds from investors and use these funds for the growth and development of the business. This helps tourism businesses diversify their funding sources and create new revenue models.

Social dimensions of blockchain and sustainable tourism

Blockchain technology also offers significant opportunities to support social sustainability in the tourism sector. Social sustainability requires that tourism activities benefit communities and promote social equity (Willie, 2019). In this context, blockchain technology provides many social benefits, such as increasing community engagement, promoting fair trade, and ensuring tourist safety. Blockchain technology has the potential to increase community engagement. Local communities in tourism destinations can directly benefit from and actively participate in tourism activities (Pilkington, 2017). For example, blockchain-based platforms can incentivize the participation of local communities in tourism projects and enable them to

72   *The Future of Blockchain in Tourism and Hospitality*

directly generate revenue from these projects. This supports the economic development of local communities and promotes social equity. Fair trade is an important component of social sustainability in the tourism sector (Tham and Sigala, 2020). Blockchain technology can be used to promote fair trade. For example, blockchain-based supply chain management systems can verify that tourism products and services are produced and distributed in accordance with fair trade principles. This allows tourists to opt for products and services that support fair trade practices and ensures that local producers and service providers are paid fairly (Pilkington, 2020). Tourist safety is another important component of social sustainability in the tourism sector. Blockchain technology can be used to ensure the safety of tourists. For example, blockchain-based authentication systems can help tourists securely verify their identities and stay safe while traveling. Furthermore, blockchain-based health information management systems allow tourists to securely manage their health information and access healthcare services when needed.

Integrating blockchain technology into sustainable tourism

The integration of blockchain technology into sustainable tourism practices brings with it a variety of challenges and opportunities. The integration of blockchain technology can involve technical and operational challenges (Dogru et al., 2018). For example, the complexity and technical requirements of blockchain technology can initially be challenging for tourism businesses. However, the security, transparency, and efficiency benefits that blockchain technology provides make overcoming these challenges worthwhile. By providing the necessary infrastructure and expertise to integrate blockchain technology, tourism businesses can take advantage of the benefits it offers (Pilkington, 2020). Integrating blockchain technology into sustainable tourism requires collaboration and cooperation. Stakeholders in the tourism sector should work together to integrate blockchain technology and develop joint strategies to maximize its potential. For example, tourism businesses, technology providers, and governments can develop joint projects for blockchain-based sustainable tourism applications and pool resources to support these projects (Bell and Hollander, 2018). Integration of blockchain technology requires education and awareness building. Tourism businesses and tourists should be made aware of the benefits and applications of blockchain

Blockchain's role in promoting sustainable tourism practices 73

technology. This ensures the adoption and mainstreaming of blockchain technology (Ludeiro, 2019). For example, tourism businesses can organize educational programs and awareness campaigns to promote the benefits and applications of blockchain technology. Furthermore, tourists should be informed about how blockchain-based sustainable tourism practices work and how they benefit them.

Blockchain technology will play an important role in the future of sustainable tourism. This technology enables the tourism sector to be more efficient, fair, and sustainable. In the future, blockchain technology is expected to be more widely used in the tourism sector (Hoffman et al., 2020). This will make the tourism sector more transparent, secure, and sustainable and will play an important role in achieving sustainable tourism goals. In the future, blockchain technology could be more widely used in smart cities and tourism applications. Smart cities can use blockchain technology for energy management, transportation, waste management, and other services, enabling tourists to have more sustainable travel experiences (Kwok and Koh, 2019). Blockchain technology can also be an important tool for sustainable tourism policies and regulations. Using blockchain-based systems, governments and policymakers can monitor and evaluate the sustainability practices of tourism businesses (Name and Choi, 2022). Global collaborations will play an important role in the future of blockchain technology in sustainable tourism. Using blockchain-based systems, stakeholders in the tourism sector can share information and resources more efficiently and support sustainable tourism practices. This makes the tourism sector more resilient and sustainable and plays an important role in achieving global sustainability goals (Caddeo and Pinna, 2021).

Blockchain technology is an important tool in achieving sustainable tourism goals. This technology enables secure, transparent, and efficient transactions in the tourism sector. Furthermore, blockchain technology plays an important role in achieving economic, social, and environmental sustainability goals. In the future, blockchain technology is expected to be more widely used in the tourism sector and contribute to the development of sustainable tourism (Treiblmaier and Önder, 2019). Therefore, it is important that stakeholders in the tourism sector understand the opportunities offered by blockchain technology and integrate it into sustainable tourism development. This is critical to building a sustainable tourism future and makes the future of tourism more equitable, transparent, and resilient.

74 *The Future of Blockchain in Tourism and Hospitality*

Challenges and opportunities in integrating blockchain for responsible tourism

Responsible tourism is an increasingly important concept in the modern travel industry. This approach to tourism focuses on minimizing travelers' impact on the places they visit by promoting economic, environmental, and social sustainability. Blockchain technology offers unique opportunities to support this important goal of tourism by providing transparency and trustworthiness (Kwok and Koh, 2018). However, the implementation of this innovative technology brings with it several challenges. This chapter examines the integration of blockchain technology into responsible tourism, exploring in depth the opportunities it offers and the challenges it faces (Name and Choi, 2022).

The biggest promise of blockchain technology is to make business processes in the tourism sector more trustworthy by increasing transparency and accountability (Willie, 2019). It can be difficult to verify whether the hotel a tourist has booked is truly eco-friendly or whether a tour operator contributes to local communities. Thanks to the immutable records offered by blockchain, all parties can trace the origin and authenticity of services. This can prevent fraud and encourage ethical practices by businesses. For example, tourists can easily verify a hotel's sustainable practices or a restaurant's local suppliers via blockchain, which supports ethical ways of doing business (Dogru et al., 2018; Kwok and Koh, 2018).

Blockchain technology can also transform transaction processes by simplifying payments and eliminating intermediaries. Traditional payment systems create challenges such as high transaction fees and delays, especially for small and local businesses (Goudarzi and Martin, 2018). Blockchain-based payment systems and cryptocurrencies can facilitate direct and low-cost transactions between tourists and local merchants. This can help support local economies and encourage financial inclusion. Especially in developing countries, blockchain can help local businesses reach a wider customer base, freeing them from the constraints of traditional financial systems (Irvin and Sullivan, 2018).

Ensuring the sustainability and ethical sourcing of products and services is critical in responsible tourism. Blockchain can ensure sustainable and ethical sourcing by tracing the journey of products from their source to the final consumer. Such a traceability system allows tourists to verify that the products they buy are indeed "green" and that

Blockchain's role in promoting sustainable tourism practices 75

the possibility of fraud is limited. For example, thanks to blockchain, a hotel can certify that the food it uses comes from organic farms, which increases tourist trust (Kwok and Koh, 2018).

Trust is a cornerstone of the tourism industry. Blockchain can increase trust by providing verifiable and immutable records of data such as service quality and customer reviews. This is especially useful in building trusted rating systems for hotels, restaurants, and attractions. Tourists can make more informed decisions based on trusted reviews and service histories. Furthermore, unique authentication systems built with blockchain prevent fake reviews and rating manipulations, creating a transparent and fair rating environment (Pilkington, 2017).

Blockchain technology can transform loyalty programs by making them more flexible and interoperable across various service providers (Willie, 2019). Tourists can accumulate and spend points across different businesses and destinations, encouraging continuous interaction with responsible tourism operators. Blockchain-based loyalty programs reduce the burden of administration and increase the security of customer rewards (Pilkington, 2017). For example, a traveler can spend the points they collect at a hotel through a loyalty program powered by blockchain technology with a restaurant or a tour operator, increasing the gains for both businesses and tourists.

Blockchain also offers significant opportunities for innovative financial solutions such as microfinancing and crowdfunding. Such platforms can provide secure and transparent mechanisms for supporting local tourism initiatives and small businesses. Blockchain-based crowdfunding platforms offer a reliable way to raise funds from tourists worldwide, which allows local communities to develop and sustain responsible tourism projects. For example, an eco-tourism project launched using blockchain technology can raise funds directly from global tourists, thus strengthening the local economy (Tham and Sigala, 2020).

Blockchain technology enables the creation of tokens that represent sustainable practices and contributions. These tokens can incentivize and reward tourists for engaging in responsible behavior. For example, a blockchain-based system could enable tourists to earn rewards for sustainable behaviors such as environmental cleanup or plastic waste collection. By gamifying sustainability efforts, such a system could make it more attractive for tourists to make responsible choices (Bell and Hollander, 2018). This, in turn, contributes to tourists developing

76 *The Future of Blockchain in Tourism and Hospitality*

eco-friendly habits while reducing the environmental footprint of their destinations. However, the integration of blockchain technology in tourism brings several challenges (Goudarzi and Martin, 2018). Technological complexity and barriers to acceptance can make it difficult to adopt this innovative technology. The tourism sector is made up of many small and medium businesses, and it can be difficult for them to adopt blockchain solutions due to a lack of technical knowledge and a lack of resources. This complexity can slow the adoption process and create barriers to entry, especially in developing regions where responsible tourism is most needed (Pilkington, 2020).

Regulatory and legal uncertainties can also pose significant barriers to blockchain and cryptocurrency adoption. Regulatory environments in different countries are still evolving and vary significantly. These uncertainties and inconsistencies can complicate the implementation of blockchain technology in tourism. Businesses may face challenges in understanding and complying with regulatory requirements, which may hinder the development and implementation of blockchain-based solutions (Irvin and Sullivan, 2018).

Blockchain networks, especially large networks such as Bitcoin and Ethereum, face scalability issues and large energy consumption. High energy requirements contradict sustainability principles, and this can undermine efforts to promote responsible tourism practices. For blockchain to align with sustainable tourism goals, it is critical to find scalable and energy-efficient solutions. This is necessary both to reduce the environmental impact of the technology and to ensure its adoption by a broad user base (Irvin and Sullivan, 2018; Name and Choi, 2022).

While blockchain offers transparency, it also raises concerns about privacy and data security. The immutable nature of blockchain means that personal and sensitive information can be permanently recorded and made accessible to anyone. This poses significant privacy risks, especially in the tourism sector, where personal data is regularly processed. How blockchain applications can secure data privacy while maintaining the benefits of transparency is a complex problem and needs to be carefully addressed (Ludeiro, 2019).

The incompatibility between different blockchain platforms and the lack of standard protocols can limit the seamless integration of blockchain solutions across the tourism ecosystem. Various stakeholders, from travel agents to local vendors, may use different blockchain technologies, creating compatibility issues and hindering

Blockchain's role in promoting sustainable tourism practices 77

the development of a unified approach to responsible tourism. Standardization efforts and open-source platforms can play an important role in creating a more cohesive and inclusive blockchain ecosystem for tourism (Caddeo and Pinna, 2021).

Implementing blockchain technology requires significant initial investments in infrastructure, development, and training. Many tourism businesses, especially small and medium enterprises and community-based projects, may struggle to underwrite these costs. Furthermore, high transaction fees on some blockchain networks can further increase operational costs. This could hinder the widespread adoption of blockchain technology in tourism and make it difficult for local businesses to take full advantage of this innovation (Bell and Hollander, 2018).

Adopting blockchain technology requires a significant shift in business operations and mindset. Stakeholders in the tourism sector may resist the adoption of new technologies, especially in regions where traditional business practices are prevalent. Cultural resistance and a lack of understanding of the benefits of blockchain can slow down the integration process and limit the impact of the technology on responsible tourism. In this context, it is crucial to educate stakeholders and disseminate the potential benefits of blockchain to the masses (Willie, 2019).

To make the most of blockchain technology's opportunities in responsible tourism and overcome the challenges, a multi-pronged approach is required. First, awareness-raising and education programs should be established for stakeholders at all levels to understand and implement the potential benefits of blockchain. Collaborative efforts should be developed among technology providers, tourism businesses, and regulatory bodies to facilitate blockchain adoption (Irvin and Sullivan, 2018). To address blockchain's energy efficiency challenges, investments should be made in more energy-efficient technologies, such as low-energy consensus mechanisms such as Proof-of-Stake (PoS). This could enable the technology to be adopted by a broad user base while reducing its environmental impact. Focus on interoperability and integration to ensure seamless integration of blockchain solutions with existing systems. Standardization efforts and open-source platforms can contribute to creating a more cohesive and inclusive blockchain ecosystem (Pilkington, 2017).

Financial incentives, subsidies, and technical support should be provided to encourage small and medium enterprises to adopt

78 *The Future of Blockchain in Tourism and Hospitality*

blockchain. By supporting such initiatives, governments and industry organizations can help local communities and businesses adopt blockchain solutions that promote responsible tourism (Dogru et al., 2018). To ensure data privacy in blockchain applications, privacy-preserving techniques such as zero-knowledge proofs and confidential transactions should be used. This can maintain trust and security by ensuring that blockchain applications comply with data protection regulations and best practices (Calvaresi et al., 2019).

Engaging local communities in the development and implementation of blockchain-based responsible tourism initiatives can increase the adoption and effectiveness of the technology. Engaging and incentivizing communities to participate in and benefit from blockchain solutions can increase acceptance and lead to more successful projects. The integration of blockchain technology in the tourism sector can be a powerful tool to promote responsible tourism practices (Dogru et al., 2018). However, a strategic approach must be taken to make the most of the opportunities offered by the technology and overcome the challenges. This approach can realize blockchain's potential to create a sustainable, fair, and responsible tourism future by increasing transparency, efficiency, and security (Larchet, 2017).

Successful integration of blockchain technology in tourism requires a long-term vision that requires the participation and collaboration of all stakeholders. This technology has the potential to revolutionize the way tourism is responsible and sustainable. However, both education about the technology and hands-on support are important to realize this potential. By enabling travelers to leave a positive impact on the places they visit, blockchain can help build a brighter future for all stakeholders in tourism (Dogru et al., 2018).

To realize the potential of blockchain, it is necessary to first invest in education and awareness-raising efforts. This education should not only reach tech enthusiasts but also small and medium businesses in the tourism sector. The tourism industry can greatly benefit from technology-based solutions, but their adoption will only be possible if the parties involved understand the technology and use it effectively. Understanding the advantages that blockchain offers and integrating them into responsible tourism practices is a valuable opportunity for travelers and businesses alike (Goudarzi and Martin, 2018).

To reduce the environmental impact of blockchain technology, energy-efficient solutions need to be developed and utilized. Energy consumption is one of the biggest criticisms of blockchain technology,

Blockchain's role in promoting sustainable tourism practices 79

and this issue can be a serious obstacle, especially in the context of sustainable tourism. Adopting energy-saving consensus mechanisms such as PoS can significantly reduce the environmental impact of blockchain. Furthermore, blockchain projects should be encouraged to develop strategies to offset and reduce energy consumption. This will ensure that the technology aligns with sustainability principles (Pilkington, 2017).

Interoperability and integration challenges must be overcome to ensure the wide adoption of blockchain in tourism. Compatibility issues among different blockchain platforms can hinder the development of uniform and inclusive solutions in the sector. Therefore, promoting open-source platforms and establishing standards can facilitate the integration of the technology. Solutions should be developed to enable different stakeholders in the tourism sector to adopt blockchain technology and integrate it with their existing systems (Bell and Hollander, 2018).

Financial incentives and technical support should be provided to small and medium enterprises to adopt blockchain technology. This can play an important role, especially in developing countries and local communities (Irvin and Sullivan, 2018). Governments, international organizations, and industry associations can offer financial support and educational programs to encourage the adoption of blockchain solutions. This will make it easier for local businesses and communities to use blockchain solutions that support responsible tourism practices (Ludeiro, 2019).

Data privacy and security are important factors to support the use of blockchain in tourism. Questions on how blockchain applications will secure data privacy while maintaining transparency need to be addressed. Integrating privacy-enhancing technologies into blockchain systems is a critical step to ensure compliance with data protection regulations. This will ensure the secure use of blockchain in the tourism sector and gain the trust of all stakeholders (Caddeo and Pinna, 2021).

Encouraging the participation of local communities in blockchain-based responsible tourism initiatives will increase the adoption and effectiveness of the technology. Engaging communities in the development and implementation of blockchain solutions allows them to directly benefit from the technology (Kwok and Koh, 2018). This not only increases the acceptance of blockchain but also makes responsible tourism initiatives more successful. To encourage the participation of

80　*The Future of Blockchain in Tourism and Hospitality*

communities in blockchain projects, solutions should be developed to address their needs and goals (Name and Choi, 2022).

The integration of blockchain technology in the tourism sector can be a powerful tool for promoting responsible tourism. A strategic approach should be adopted to make the most of the opportunities offered by the technology and overcome the challenges. This approach can realize blockchain's potential to create a sustainable, fair, and responsible tourism future by increasing transparency, efficiency, and security. By fostering innovation and development in the tourism sector, blockchain can contribute to a more sustainable and ethical tourism model that meets the needs of travelers and local communities (Kwok and Koh, 2018).

The integration of blockchain into responsible tourism, as in many sectors, has the potential to create far-reaching impacts. Blockchain not only transforms transaction processes but also makes the tourism experience more transparent, trustworthy, and ethical. This technology offers solutions that benefit both travelers and local communities, making it easier for tourism to achieve its sustainability goals (Willie, 2019). Exploring the opportunities offered by blockchain and overcoming the challenges is key to future-proofing the tourism industry. It is therefore essential that all stakeholders in the industry collaborate to maximize the potential of blockchain technology and support the development of sustainable, responsible tourism (Pilkington, 2017).

Case study: Using blockchain to support sustainable tourism initiatives globally

In recent years, blockchain technology has become an important tool in achieving sustainability goals by providing innovative solutions in the tourism sector as well as in many other sectors. Many tourism destinations around the world are supporting and developing sustainable tourism practices using blockchain technology. In this section, we will explore a few global examples of how blockchain technology is supporting sustainable tourism initiatives.

Winding tree decentralized reservation system

Winding Tree is one of the most well-known applications of blockchain technology in the tourism sector. This platform offers a decentralized booking system for hotels, airlines, and other travel service providers.

Blockchain's role in promoting sustainable tourism practices 81

Unlike traditional booking systems, Winding Tree reduces costs by eliminating intermediaries and providing a more transparent booking process. This offers a fairer and more sustainable system for both tourism businesses and tourists. Furthermore, recording transactions on the blockchain helps prevent fake bookings and fraud attempts, which contributes to increased trust in the industry.

Grin: Crypto donation platform for sustainable tourism

Grin offers an innovative way to fund sustainable tourism projects using blockchain technology. The platform enables tourists and investors to donate to sustainable tourism projects through cryptocurrencies. Donations can be tracked transparently on the blockchain, which allows donors to see how their money is being used. This helps sustainable tourism projects receive more support and contributes to the economic development of communities. Furthermore, Grin enables local communities to directly benefit from tourism and sustainability initiatives to reach a wider audience.

Bext360: Sustainable supply chain management

Bext360 supports sustainable supply chain management in the tourism sector using blockchain technology. The platform monitors the supply chain of tourism products and services and verifies that these processes comply with sustainability criteria. For example, a hotel can use the Bext360 platform to prove that the food and beverages it uses come from sustainable sources and are produced in accordance with fair trade principles. This allows tourists to make informed choices and contributes to the mainstreaming of sustainable tourism practices.

Aloha: Blockchain-based community engagement

Aloha aims to increase the participation of local communities in tourism projects in tourism destinations using blockchain technology. The platform enables local communities to contribute to tourism projects and generate direct revenue from these projects. For example, local artists in a tourism destination can offer their works for sale on the Aloha platform and receive the proceeds from these sales securely on the blockchain. This helps support the local economy, and communities directly benefit from tourism. Furthermore, Aloha enables

82 The Future of Blockchain in Tourism and Hospitality

tourists to get to know local culture and communities better, which strengthens the social dimension of sustainable tourism.

Impact travel alliance: Sustainable tourism education

Impact Travel Alliance runs sustainable tourism education and awareness-raising projects using blockchain technology. This platform offers blockchain-based educational programs for tourism businesses and tourists. The educational programs teach sustainable tourism practices and how blockchain technology supports these practices. For example, tourists can learn about sustainable travel methods and ways to support local communities through blockchain-based education programs. This contributes to the proliferation of sustainable tourism and increased conscious behavior in the tourism industry.

These case studies showcase how blockchain technology is supporting sustainable tourism initiatives and its potential. Decentralized booking systems such as Winding Tree, crypto donation platforms such as Grin, sustainable supply chain management systems such as Bext360, community engagement projects such as Aloha, and education initiatives such as Impact Travel Alliance illustrate the various application areas of blockchain technology in sustainable tourism. These examples demonstrate how blockchain technology offers innovative solutions in the tourism sector and is an effective tool for achieving sustainability goals. In the future, we can expect blockchain technology to be more widely used in the tourism sector and contribute more to the development of sustainable tourism. This will make the tourism sector more fair, transparent, and sustainable.

5 Future trends and challenges

Emerging trends in blockchain and tourism

Although blockchain technology (BCT) is still in its early stages of development, its potential for enhancing service quality, guest satisfaction, and profitability in various hospitality sectors is becoming increasingly evident. Research by Dogru, Mody, and Leonardi (2018) highlights the potential applications of blockchain in hotels, restaurants, airlines, and travel agencies. By leveraging BCT, businesses can streamline operations, improve transparency, and enhance trust among stakeholders. For example, blockchain can facilitate secure and transparent transactions, provide immutable records of guest interactions, and enable efficient management of loyalty programs. As more businesses within the hospitality industry recognize the benefits of blockchain adoption, there is a growing momentum toward its implementation (Figure 5.1). This shift toward BCT has the potential to benefit all stakeholders involved, including businesses, employees, and customers, by fostering greater efficiency, reliability, and trust in the hospitality sector. In the subsequent section, we investigate the potential uses of BCT within the hospitality sector, focusing on emerging trends in blockchain and tourism (Mujačević, 2024).

Payment services

The tourism industry, as highlighted by Gössling (2021) and Cai et al. (2019), is characterized by its dynamic nature and readiness to embrace innovation, as evidenced by the integration of new technologies. Cryptocurrencies and blockchains have emerged as transformative forces, offering innovative solutions for the tourism

DOI: 10.4324/9781003521617-6

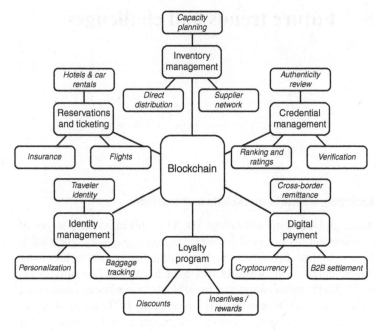

Figure 5.1 Key blockchain applications for advancing tourism.

Source: Mujačević (2024).

sector. This technological evolution necessitates a keen awareness of shifting tourism demands to maintain competitiveness. Takale et al. (2024) explain that BCT simplifies payment processes by removing numerous intermediaries typically present in transaction processing. Real-time payment verification using blockchain data facilitates quick confirmation and recording of transactions, thereby enhancing transparency and security in cross-border payments.

Researchers, as evidenced by studies conducted by Pilkington et al. (2017), Jain et al. (2023), Aiazbekov (2023), and Gültekin (2017), are increasingly exploring the application of cryptocurrencies, particularly Bitcoin, and the economic possibilities presented by BCT in tourism and hospitality. These studies delve into various aspects of this burgeoning field, including the impact of cryptocurrencies on tourism demand and consumer behavior. Quan et al. (2023) found differences in the levels of trust between Chinese and Korean consumers

Future trends and challenges 85

regarding cryptocurrency payments, with American consumers displaying higher levels of trust, as indicated by a study conducted by Nuryyev et al. (2021) assert that Bitcoin and other cryptocurrencies have emerged as decentralized forms of currency, providing insights into the implications of integrating cryptocurrency payments within the hospitality industry. Radic et al. (2022) examine the determinants influencing hospitality businesses' inclination toward adopting new digital payment methods, emphasizing perceived security as a significant predictor of technology acceptance. Treiblmaier et al. (2021) highlight the benefits of cryptocurrencies, such as their universal acceptance and minimal transaction fees, corresponding with the growing need for improved mobility among travelers. Barreto et al. (2019) assert that blockchain technologies and cryptocurrencies have significantly impacted economies, with regions such as Latin America and the Caribbean exploring cryptocurrency payments to enhance competitiveness and address poverty concerns.

Thus, introducing coins or tokens as payment methods has the potential to create a more equitable market structure and facilitate the development of effective reward systems for travelers contributing feedback on online review platforms (Nam et al., 2022). BCT can streamline tax compliance by allowing tax authorities to publicly disclose tax structures, while smart contracts can automate tax transfers and provide entities with proof of compliance (HTNG, 2018).

Additionally, blockchain-enabled e-commerce platforms offer innovative solutions, such as depositing digital coins into employees' digital wallets, granting them greater autonomy in expenditure decisions compared to traditional benefits (Ying et al., 2018). KrisPay presents a novel approach to reward redemption within the airline industry. Acting as a digital wallet, it enables Singapore Airlines customers to convert their KrisFlyer miles into usable units of payment. This innovative system empowers travelers to utilize their accumulated miles for purchases at a variety of partner merchants across Singapore, ranging from gas stations to beauty product retailers, offering a diverse array of redemption options.

On the other hand, Winding Tree, a Switzerland-based private company, is pioneering the democratization of online bookings through BCT. By leveraging blockchain, Winding Tree aims to challenge established players like Expedia and Priceline by creating a more equitable and competitive travel distribution market. A key feature of Winding Tree's platform is its ability to facilitate payments

86 *The Future of Blockchain in Tourism and Hospitality*

in local currencies, promoting local spending and economic growth. Through its LÍF token, Winding Tree endeavors to establish direct connections between travelers and service providers, thereby reducing fees for travelers and cutting costs for service providers alike. This approach aims to foster greater accessibility and affordability within the travel industry while promoting financial inclusivity and efficiency.

Therefore, BCT offers several methods to ensure payment security in the travel industry. Firstly, it creates an unchangeable record of transactions, making it challenging for travelers to dispute charges as banks or credit card companies can easily verify purchases. Secondly, blockchain enables fast and secure payment processing by allowing direct transactions between parties without intermediaries like banks, thereby reducing transaction times and costs. Lastly, the integration of blockchain into payment systems in the travel sector highlights its role in enhancing security, efficiency, and transparency in financial transactions, fostering trust and reliability among travelers and service providers.

Booking and reservations

In the travel industry, various online booking agencies play a dominant role by connecting customers with services like hotels, boat charters, and leisure activities. These agencies typically charge a minimum commission of 15%, which increases the cost of the services for both customers and providers. However, in decentralized booking markets, these intermediaries are bypassed, allowing tourism service providers to directly interact with travelers. This eliminates the need for intermediaries and ensures transparent transactions, pricing, and potential fees, leading to a more favorable experience for tourists (Halkiopoulos, Antonopoulou, and Kostopoulos, 2023).

According to Maythu et al. (2024), BCT allows hotels and travelers to make transactions directly without intermediaries, which lowers expenses. It also automates booking procedures, decreasing the chance of double bookings. Furthermore, the unchangeable nature of blockchain records builds trust and responsibility because all transaction details are kept secure, reducing the risk of fraud and improving the booking experience for both hotels and guests. Examples of companies using this approach include Winding Tree and Nordic Choice Hotels.

Future trends and challenges 87

Furthermore, BCT, as highlighted by Treiblmaier (2022), can simplify the reservation and ticketing process and help eliminate unauthorized ticket sales. This can be achieved by establishing a common ticketing protocol where buyers can verify ticket ownership using their digital wallets. If a ticket is transferred to someone else, the original ticket is voided, and a new one is issued (Larchet, 2017). Similarly, managing airline ticketing, which involves multiple stakeholders, can be streamlined with blockchain solutions (Goudarzi and Martin, 2018).

As for Caddo and Pinna (2021), BCT can be valuable for various purposes such as making reservations, issuing tickets, and combating illicit markets. For instance, there's an Italian startup that introduced an app called WICKET, which utilizes a blockchain-based protocol to digitize tickets and prevent speculation. This app employs the GET (Guaranteed Entrance Token) protocol, already in use in the Netherlands and Singapore for selling tickets to sports events, concerts, fairs, and conferences. Recently, in response to the global pandemic, the app proposed a solution for beach establishments to allow beachgoers to book their spots online and pay securely. The system links each ticket to the buyer's phone number, generating a unique QR code stored in a special app wallet for easy access to the facility.

Lastly, airlines face challenges in maintaining schedules, handling weather and technical issues, while also maximizing capacity and ensuring customer loyalty. Akmeemana (2017) highlights the frequent issue of having more ticketed passengers at the departure gate than there are seats on the plane. Passengers naturally expect the seat they purchased to be available. To ensure flights are fully booked, airlines often overbook. However, this can become expensive when all passengers arrive, forcing gate staff to handle the overflow and find accommodations for everyone. Thus, BCT can alleviate some of these burdens by expediting security checks, verifying passenger documentation, and enhancing booking accuracy to prevent false or duplicate bookings.

Loyalty programs

According to Yin et al. (2019), incorporating BCT into loyalty programs enables companies and customers to resolve any disagreements regarding loyalty points. These blockchain-based loyalty programs are both verifiable and secure.

88   *The Future of Blockchain in Tourism and Hospitality*

Treiblmaier (2022) elucidated that numerous current loyalty programs suffer from administrative intricacies and a deficiency in effectively communicating benefits to customers. Consequently, a substantial portion of accrued points often goes unredeemed. This uncertainty about when points or miles will be redeemed results in accrued but unrecognized expenses (Irvin and Sullivan, 2018).

Introducing loyalty tokens that can be freely traded would establish a competitive market, providing organizations with valuable feedback on their performance (Dogru et al., 2018). These tokens offer versatility across different industries. Hence, the use of loyalty wallets for tracking tokens across partners and transaction types facilitates seamless connectivity and real-time processing, enabling efficient point exchanges and coordination through smart contracts while ensuring a comprehensive audit trail (Irvin and Sullivan, 2018).

Common loyalty program transactions facilitated on a blockchain include point transfers between accounts, point exchanges across programs, and bundled redemption offers across multiple partners (HTNG, 2018). The aggregation of information from various loyalty programs also presents opportunities for companies to enhance personalized marketing efforts, although this may raise privacy concerns among consumers.

The concept of using blockchain for loyalty programs is not entirely new, as the first application of blockchain was to support a non-governmental currency, like Bitcoin. Airlines have long used non-governmental currency in the form of loyalty miles. By tokenizing air miles on the blockchain, passengers could securely pay for goods and services without involving third-party credit card processors. Similar to current air miles programs, tokens could be acquired for future use or exchanged for non-ticket items. Accumulated and unused points pose a liability for airlines, with approximately 17.5 trillion unused air miles currently. Airlines are attempting to mitigate this liability by increasing redemption requirements, introducing expiration dates, or promoting the use of points for non-flight purposes. For instance, Singapore Airlines' KrisPay loyalty program transforms flying miles into cryptocurrency and securely stores them in customers' digital wallets.

Early adoption of blockchain-based solutions in loyalty programs could help program owners manage the accounting challenges posed by unredeemed rewards, while offering customers benefits through alternative redemption channels and improving customer knowledge.

Future trends and challenges 89

Consolidating programs under a major airline or hotel chain could enhance the customer experience. However, cooperative programs also entail the risk of data pooling and sharing, giving early adopters a competitive advantage in shaping program structures. Just as online travel agencies disrupted flight booking processes, disruptors in the loyalty sector could challenge program operators by introducing cost-effective solutions, potentially leading to loss of airline membership and fees (Akmeemana, 2017).

Customer loyalty and engagement are critical factors that can significantly impact the success of companies across various industries. Reward programs are considered strategic investments for organizations of all types. Despite their rapid growth, these programs often suffer from inefficiencies. However, BCT has emerged as a powerful solution to unlock the full potential of customer loyalty programs. Organizations, including banks and airlines, can benefit from the efficiencies, cost reductions, and enhanced brand loyalty that blockchain offers. The diversity of reward programs, such as airline loyalty programs, underscores their importance for both businesses and consumers. Extensive literature highlights the benefits of loyalty programs for businesses, including customer retention, acquisition, and increasing customer lifetime value. Loyalty programs also foster brand advocacy, enable responsive pricing strategies, and reduce promotional costs (Bolton, Kannan and Bramlett, 2000; Dowling and Uncles, 1997; Schatsky and Muraskin, 2015; Lewis, 2004). By leveraging BCT, businesses can streamline their operations and achieve efficiency-driven profits (Lowenstein, 2002; Clark, 2010; Wener, 2004).

Typically, travel industry businesses provide loyalty rewards to their customers, such as airline miles or complimentary stays. However, many users find these reward systems restrictive. Digital tokens offer an opportunity to enhance the security, transferability, and transparency of these rewards. By integrating tokens into loyalty programs and transitioning them into a decentralized value network, customers can now select their preferred rewards. This approach ensures that products and services from different companies are transparent and comparable, allows for easy transfer of rewards between programs, and enables reward points to be converted into digital assets (Banerji et al., 2021).

Operators in the travel industry can gain advantages from establishing specialized loyalty programs that distribute tokens as rewards to travelers. Evidence suggests that companies employing such systems can gain a competitive edge over rivals, attract new potential customers, and enhance brand perception, thereby strengthening the connection between travelers and destinations. For instance, the startup Loyal has introduced a blockchain-based platform enabling companies to manage their loyalty programs through various reward schemes. The Arab Group Jumeirah, in partnership with Dubai Holding, utilizes this platform to enhance the effectiveness of its loyalty programs. Conversely, Trippki has developed a loyalty program facilitating direct interaction between customers and tourism sector companies, thereby promoting sectoral disintermediation. Specifically, customers receive tokens (recorded in the blockchain without expiry) for staying at specific hotels, ensuring the ability to redeem them at any time (Caddeo and Pinna, 2021).

Loyalty programs can sometimes lead to more issues than solutions. Hotels and airlines have started using BCT to create loyalty programs, issuing loyalty tokens as rewards to their guests (Kowalewski, McLaughlin, and Hill, 2017; Kowalewski and Simon, 2016). These loyalty tokens work similarly to loyalty points, but BCT allows customers to freely buy, sell, or trade their loyalty tokens with others. Allowing customers to exchange loyalty points openly can make loyalty programs more competitive and improve overall service quality. For instance, the market value of tokens from one company may be higher than another due to the quality of products or services they can purchase. This encourages companies to improve their offerings to attract more customers, benefiting the entire system. Additionally, loyalty tokens could be used across different industries, allowing consumers to use their hotel loyalty tokens at restaurants, airlines, coffee shops, and other businesses through a blockchain platform. In partnership with IBM, startup technology company Loyyal is developing a blockchain platform where consumers can redeem, purchase, sell, or exchange their loyalty points (Hill and Brierley, 2017).

Identity protection and privacy safeguarding

In the future, the exchange of identity data among various entities and even across different blockchain networks could lead to the creation of a universal traveler identity (Bell and Hollander, 2018). This could effectively combat identity theft, which is particularly concerning for travelers who frequently need to present their identification for various

Future trends and challenges 91

purposes such as boarding flights, checking into hotels, renting cars, or buying alcohol.

Traditional identity verification methods often expose personal information to both authorized individuals and onlookers. However, utilizing IDs containing cryptographically secured codes can enable identity verification without divulging personal details (Dogru et al., 2018). Streamlining identity verification processes would also benefit professionals in the tourism industry, such as airline staff (Goudarzi and Martin, 2018).

A blockchain-based identity solution can ensure the selective sharing of data in compliance with relevant laws. Additionally, biometric data like fingerprints, iris scans, and facial recognition can be incorporated to meet the requirements of different authorities. By storing all this information on the blockchain, hotels could simplify their operations by eliminating the need to report guest arrivals to law enforcement or immigration authorities, instead recording arrival and departure dates directly on the blockchain (HTNG, 2018).

Chami Akmeemana (2017) underscores the importance of establishing digital identities for various stakeholders in aviation, including passengers, pilots, airport personnel, equipment, and aircraft parts. BCT, if correctly implemented, offers a solution to securely share information globally while maintaining user privacy, as emphasized by Armin Ebrahimi, CEO and founder of ShoCard. This advancement holds the potential to revolutionize identity management.

In practical terms, each unique digital ID corresponds to a specific entity, mirroring real-world interactions. For example, individuals' digital identities encompass personal details such as education, job credentials, past purchases, and travel and hotel reservations. By recording these transactions on a blockchain, individuals create an immutable, timestamped record due to the interconnected nature of the blockchain. Any attempt to tamper with the data would be rejected by network nodes, safeguarding the integrity of the chain. Moreover, the integration of digital IDs with reservations facilitates automatic linkage to loyalty programs, providing airlines with comprehensive insights into their customers and unlocking new revenue opportunities.

According to Dogru, Mody, and Leonardi (2018), BCT holds promise as a solution to identity theft. In various settings such as airports, hotels, and restaurants, customers frequently need to present their IDs for verification purposes, exposing them to the risk of identity theft. This vulnerability arises not only from those checking IDs but

92 *The Future of Blockchain in Tourism and Hospitality*

also from bystanders who may gain access to sensitive personal information. To address this risk, IDs, including birth certificates, driver's licenses, social security numbers, and passports, among others, can be securely stored on a blockchain platform. Individuals can then be granted permissions to verify and validate these IDs (Davidson, De Filippi, and Potts, 2016). Similar to QR codes, IDs can be represented by cryptographically secured codes, enabling identity verification without disclosing sensitive personal information. Storing digital IDs on a blockchain not only reduces the risk of physical ID loss or theft but also mitigates the possibility of forgery (Gupta, 2017).

Viewed from an alternate angle, Riechmann (2020) highlights the common inconvenience of long queues and unpleasant experiences encountered by travelers before and after flights. Throughout the customer journey, there are numerous instances where travelers must verify and share their identity to comply with legal requirements and access services. This often involves interaction with multiple intermediary parties such as airlines, airports, customs, and immigration authorities, each independently verifying customer identities. This decentralized process results in significant time consumption, inefficiency, and dissatisfaction for travelers.

BCT offers a potential solution by connecting the various stakeholders involved in the identity verification process. Instead of repeatedly validating a passenger's identity at every touchpoint, blockchain could facilitate a one-time validation at the outset of the journey, potentially linked to biometric data, serving as a unique identifier throughout. Relevant entities would be granted access to traveler data, enabling seamless movement within the ecosystem. Additionally, supplementary travel documentation like visas could be directly associated with passenger identity, facilitating easy access for relevant authorities.

By automating and centralizing the validation of passenger identities, this solution has the potential to enhance efficiency and reduce the time required for traveler validation across the customer journey. Moreover, it could mitigate instances where passengers without valid visas mistakenly board flights, leading to costly repatriation and fees for airlines. A blockchain system providing comprehensive information on all necessary travel documents could prevent such occurrences, benefiting both travelers and airlines. This streamlined process would significantly reduce queue times, enhancing the overall travel experience for customers and allowing for smoother navigation through

Future trends and challenges 93

checkpoints from departure to arrival. Leveraging blockchain's capability to facilitate decentralized, secure, and trustworthy data access, this solution enhances data transferability across the entire passenger identity ecosystem (Riechmann, 2020).

BCT, utilizing a zero-knowledge protocol (zero-knowledge proof), allows the recording of identity documents without exposing sensitive information. This facilitates public tracking of individuals throughout their journeys, leading to savings in time and money. Consequently, blockchain has made significant inroads into the tourism sector, with major players such as Marriott, TUI, AXA, and others adopting the technology to enhance the protection and efficiency of tourism services across various domains (Li et al., 2021).

Caddeo and Pinna (2021) propose enhancing sector safety and protecting travelers' privacy by establishing a digital global traveler identity system. This system would accurately determine a person's identity, thus addressing the issue of identity theft frequently encountered by tourists. For instance, incorporating biometric information such as fingerprints and facial recognition alongside other registered details could streamline hotel operations. Hotels would only need to record guests' arrival and departure dates on the blockchain, eliminating the requirement to report to law enforcement or other authorities.

Additionally, SITA (*International Air Transport Telecommunications Society*), the telecommunications company of air transport, is exploring the use of virtual or digital passports to reduce document checks during passenger journeys. By storing biometric data and other personal information in a single token on mobile or wearable devices, travelers could be swiftly identified by any authority with just one interaction. Thus, the anticipated rise in passenger numbers underscores the ongoing challenge of ensuring reliable passenger identification, particularly in the context of heightened safety concerns where even minor lapses in airline and airport security can lead to serious consequences. Efficient and secure passenger identification offers multiple benefits: it allows for verification of details during reservation, reducing the need for manual checks by TSA or border agents and shortening queues; facilitates communication of customer requirements such as special assistance or dietary needs through a comprehensive data bundle; enables airlines to tailor offers to potential customers based on their preferences, thereby securing business without engaging in price competition; and enhances revenue integrity

94　*The Future of Blockchain in Tourism and Hospitality*

by associating each booking with a digital ID, ultimately leading to fuller flights and increased profitability (Akmeemana, 2017).

Enhancing logistics: Tracking air cargo, luggage, guests, and food products

BCT offers significant potential for enhancing various aspects of travel and logistics, including real-time air cargo tracking and baggage tracing. By leveraging the immutable ledger provided by blockchain, the movement of baggage throughout its journey can be meticulously recorded, from its point of origin to its final destination, as well as any intermediate stops along the way (Maythu et al., 2024).

Expanding on this notion of traceability, BCT can also be applied to track tourists' personal belongings during their travels. Baggage issues generally fall into three categories: stolen bags, damage or destruction of bags or their contents, and delayed bags due to various airport infrastructure issues. A study by Akmeemana (2017) highlights that while luggage loss rates have reached historically low levels and continue to decline annually, there are still 5.73 mishandled bags per 1000 passengers, totaling 21.6 million cases, according to SITA.

Currently, passengers lack a means to track their luggage personally after check-in, although emerging technologies like personal sensors and RFID solutions show promise. Thus, lost luggage is a recurring issue in the travel industry, causing inconvenience for both passengers and businesses. (Jiang et al., 2023) pointed out that the issue of lost luggage persists because of the involvement of multiple parties in baggage handling during travel. Although airlines have made some improvements in this area, many travelers continue to face difficulties with lost baggage.

BCT offers an optimistic solution by providing a decentralized and transparent system for tracking baggage. Through blockchain, stakeholders can easily find luggage without the need for complex databases. Additionally, in response to the persistent challenge of lost luggage, advancements in baggage tracking technology have emerged, further harnessing the advantages of blockchain (Halkiopoulos, Antonopoulou, and Kostopoulos, 2023). For example, systems like Bagtrax utilize sensors attached to luggage, enabling travelers to monitor their belongings during transfers and promptly request compensation if needed. By utilizing BCT, these systems ensure the security of tracking data and safeguard the information of all involved

Future trends and challenges 95

stakeholders, including passengers, airlines, airport authorities, and insurance companies (Caddeo and Pinna, 2021). Thus, blockchain-enabled baggage tracking systems not only simplify the process of locating lost luggage but also improve overall efficiency and security within the travel industry.

Moreover, BCT has applications in inventory management systems, which in the hospitality sector can involve tracking the availability of hotel rooms or airplane seats (Dogru, Mody and Leonardi, 2018). It provides real-time information on availability and coverage rates, which can be shared with stakeholders, eliminating the need for Property Management Systems (PMS) and Central Reservation Systems (CRS) and reducing intermediary costs. For instance, the Swiss platform Winding Tree allows hoteliers and airlines to list their available accommodations for tourists to book directly. Similarly, the German group TUI is developing "BedSwap" to manage hotel room inventory more effectively in the markets it serves. Additionally, the Dubai Department of Tourism and Commerce launched "Tourism 2.0" to enhance Dubai's status as a global travel destination. This system enables checking hotel occupancy and room rates, aiding tour operators in preparing offers for customers more efficiently.

Besides, hotels can benefit from real-time updates on guests' journeys from their departure to their arrival at the hotel, improving efficiency by minimizing check-in delays and boosting guest contentment. While some may perceive tracking guests' movements as an invasion of privacy, obtaining this data will necessitate the guest's permission. Guests will retain control over the extent of information disclosed to hotels or other network participants. As a result, BCT holds promise for providing seamlessly integrated guest services while safeguarding guest privacy (Dogru, Mody and Leonardi, 2018).

Ensuring transparency in the food supply chain is of utmost importance for destinations in today's contemporary tourism landscape, especially for sectors such as food and wine tourism, which prioritize organic, local, and sustainable products (Caddeo and Pinna, 2021). BCT emerges as a valuable tool to establish a system enabling individuals to access data about the origin of food products and track their journey from farm to table. This emphasis on traceability ensures that consumers can make informed choices about the food they consume, aligning with growing concerns about health, sustainability, and ethical consumption.

96 *The Future of Blockchain in Tourism and Hospitality*

This process typically involves scanning QR codes or barcodes on products using devices linked to the blockchain. For example, Food Chain, an Italian system incorporating the Internet of Things (IoT), utilizes BCT to track food products, allowing end consumers to access information via QR codes on product packaging, thus enhancing consumer confidence through increased transparency (Caddeo and Pinna, 2021). Moreover, ensuring the tracking and monitoring of food is crucial in the restaurant industry, where food originates from the supply chain, beginning at the farm.

By extending blockchain-based supply chain management systems to restaurants, improved quality control and food safety can be achieved. Restaurants can collaborate with their food suppliers to engage in a blockchain platform that tracks and monitors food throughout its journey. Furthermore, restaurants can leverage BCT to enable their guests to trace the origins and routes of the food used in their meals, fostering trust by providing transparency regarding the quality of ingredients used in meal preparation (Dogru, Mody, and Leonardi, 2018).

Thus, blockchain systems offer transparency, allowing travelers to monitor their belongings' whereabouts and condition by documenting custody changes. This enables real-time updates on the location of their assets directly to their mobile devices (Goudarzi and Martin, 2018; Ludeiro, 2019). Consequently, blockchain proves to be a versatile tool for improving logistical operations and enhancing the travel experience itself.

Smart contracts

Leveraging blockchain-driven smart contracts can enhance organizations' auditing and reporting capabilities, thus improving service quality (Maythu et al., 2024). For instance, TUI utilizes smart contracts and private blockchains to manage room inventories, facilitating immediate payment upon transaction recording based on contractual terms. This promotes collaboration between hotels and travel agencies. Moreover, digital keys stored on the blockchain can assign hotel rooms to guests upon payment of the room rate, simplifying the check-in process. Similarly, apartments, office spaces, and cars can utilize blockchain-controlled locks for efficient access management (Maythu et al., 2024).

Future trends and challenges 97

In the airline industry, complexities in revenue recognition are addressed by sharing rules defined by IATA and executed through smart contracts, potentially leading to innovative revenue streams and accelerated revenue distribution (Irvin and Sullivan, 2018). Smart contracts also streamline flight insurance processes by automatically disbursing agreed sums in case of delays or cancellations (Dogru et al., 2018).

Additionally, the food service industry benefits from smart contracts for various purposes such as inventory procurement standing orders, support services, kitchen maintenance, and equipment purchasing or leasing (Willie, 2019). Smart contracts also hold promise in guest services, potentially revolutionizing the traditional check-in process. Through BCT, where digital IDs and authorized payment accounts are securely stored, hotel rooms can be allocated to guests, with a digital key recorded in the blockchain upon payment receipt. Notably, both IDs and payment information are encrypted for security. For instance, Slock.it, a German startup, is developing blockchain-based locks for properties, allowing renters to book and access rental properties based on predetermined terms (Gupta, 2017).

Furthermore, smart contracts can streamline travel insurance processes in case of flight delays or cancellations, with contractual terms stored in the blockchain executed automatically in such instances. Several companies in the hospitality and travel sectors are embracing BCT for various purposes. For instance, TUI Group utilizes blockchain to manage inventory distribution and internal processes (Watkins, 2017). As the industry remains optimistic about its future, blockchain's potential to deliver cheaper, better, and faster experiences attracts interest and investment across the board (Bujarski, 2018; Dogru, Mody, and Leonardi, 2018).

Online customer reviews

Another application of BCT, not limited to the hotel and air industry, involves improving online customer reviews of various tourism products, such as hotels, restaurants, flights, and events (Calvaresi et al., 2019). Technological systems that can verify the authenticity of reviews and prevent manipulation by hoteliers or consumers are in demand. However, ensuring the reliability of individual reviews is challenging, as unfair or biased reviews cannot be

98 *The Future of Blockchain in Tourism and Hospitality*

removed once posted (Nam et al., 2022). Online customer reviews play a crucial role in the tourism industry, yet their authenticity and reliability often raise doubts. Certifying reviews before storing them on the blockchain, achieved by signing them with a private key, could enhance the perceived credibility of online feedback (Pilkington, 2017).

Thus, BCT offers a transformative potential for the tourism industry, with the promise of enhancing guest experiences, streamlining operations, and lowering costs. Its impact spans across various facets, including the implementation of smart contracts, the evolution of loyalty programs, and the facilitation of secure digital payments, fundamentally changing the dynamics of interaction between businesses and travelers. Notably, established industry leaders like TUI are already integrating blockchain into their operations, while startups globally are pioneering innovative solutions. With its capacity to remove intermediaries and empower smaller enterprises, blockchain is fundamentally reshaping the tourism landscape, ushering in a decentralized and efficient ecosystem. As a result, Table 5.1 provides a detailed overview of emerging trends at the nexus of BCT and the tourism sector.

Table 5.1 Emerging trends in blockchain and tourism

Use case	Blockchain implication
Digital payment – Cryptocurrency payments	Utilizing digital currencies such as Bitcoin or Ethereum for purchasing travel services, including flights and accommodations, via online platforms or payment gateways that support cryptocurrency transactions.
Travel loyalty programs	Travel-related businesses, such as airlines, hotels, and car rental companies, provide reward programs to encourage customer loyalty by offering points or miles for purchases, which can be exchanged for benefits like free flights, hotel stays, upgrades, and other perks.

Future trends and challenges **99**

Table 5.1 (Continued)

Use case	Blockchain implication
Booking and reservations	Leveraging blockchain technology to securely store and oversee reservation data, enhancing transparency and efficiency while reducing dependency on intermediaries.
Identity protection and privacy safeguarding	Minimizing the threat of identity theft in travel transactions while enabling convenient verification without disclosing personal information, benefiting both tourists and industry professionals.
Tracking air cargo	Using blockchain technology to monitor and trace the movement of air cargo shipments from their starting point to their destination, ensuring transparent and secure tracking throughout the journey.
Luggage tracking	Blockchain technology facilitates transparent tracking of tourists' belongings by documenting custody changes, enabling travelers to receive instant updates on their items' whereabouts through their mobile devices.
Tracking guests	Track and oversee guest movements and interactions within the hospitality sector, ensuring transparent and efficient management of guest activities, preferences, and transactions during their stay.
Traceability of food products	Blockchain enables clear tracking of food products from their origin to consumers, ensuring precision and responsibility in the supply chain.

(Continued)

100　*The Future of Blockchain in Tourism and Hospitality*

Table 5.1 (Continued)

Use case	Blockchain implication
Inventory management	Offering up-to-date availability details for hotel rooms or airline seats, bypassing conventional systems such as Property Management Systems (PMS) and cutting intermediary expenses in the hospitality sector.
Smart contracts	Blockchain technology employing smart contracts automates and enforces agreements in travel transactions, streamlining processes such as booking accommodations and managing loyalty rewards, thereby boosting trust and efficiency in the sector.
Online customer reviews	Blockchain seeks to improve the authenticity and transparency of online reviews by verifying their legitimacy and addressing concerns regarding manipulation.

Challenges and considerations for widespread blockchain adoption in the tourism sector

The discussion surrounding challenges and barriers in the adoption and implementation of BCT encompasses a wide array of factors, as highlighted by various researchers.

Maythu, Kwok, and Pei-Lee (2024) identify several key challenges in BCT, including issues with technology maturity and scalability, a shortage of skilled workers, the need for user involvement, tendencies toward monopolization, perceived lack of benefits, and environmental impact. Kim (2020) categorizes these challenges as a trilemma associated with blockchain technologies, which includes scalability, security, and decentralization.

Acikgoz, Stylos, and Lythreati (2024) stress the importance of technological, organizational, and environmental constraints that hinder blockchain adoption. Filimonau and Naumova (2020) discuss challenges such as initial investment and operational costs, regulatory uncertainties, and transaction speeds.

Future trends and challenges 101

Dadkhah, Rahimnia, and Filimonau (2022) delve into societal, technical, financial, and legal challenges related to BCT, ranging from lack of awareness and education to scalability issues, energy consumption, and regulatory hurdles. Rodrigo et al. (2020) highlight workflow complexities, low business efficiency, business entity segmentation, and inadequate personal information protection.

Wang et al. (2021) classify challenges into technical, management, and legal domains, while Melnychenko et al. (2019) emphasize the lack of regulatory frameworks, technology immaturity, shortage of skilled professionals, limited awareness, societal distrust, and inadequate scientific research. Furthermore, Dogru, Mody, and Leonardi (2018) identify technical issues such as throughput, bandwidth, latency, and energy consumption within blockchain networks, along with the threat of block obstruction attacks. Rana, Adamashvili, and Tricase (2022) contribute by discussing technical issues, lack of research and examples, relevant legislation, and the importance of interoperability and collaboration.

In this section, our objective is to offer a comprehensive analysis of the diverse array of challenges that BCT encounters within the dynamic landscape of the tourism sector. Through a meticulous examination, we will delve deeply into these challenges, drawing upon the invaluable insights and perspectives provided by esteemed scholars and researchers in the field. In this context, our exploration will draw extensively from the scholarly works of Dadkhah, Rahimnia, and Filimonau (2022), as their elucidations provide a holistic understanding of the predominant dimensions of challenges, particularly encompassing societal, technical, financial, and legal challenges.

Technical challenges

The tourism industry's hesitation in fully embracing blockchain stems partly from its inability to effectively address operational demands. Despite emerging over a decade ago, blockchain integration within tourism operations remains at an early stage, primarily due to scalability concerns and the lack of compatibility among blockchain tools and services (Maythu, Kwok, and Pei-Lee, 2024). This technological immaturity, indicating the early stages of development and limited capabilities, further complicates blockchain adoption in the tourism sector (Erol et al., 2022; Acikgoz, Stylos, and Lythreati, 2024).

102   *The Future of Blockchain in Tourism and Hospitality*

Therefore, scalability emerges as a critical issue, as evidenced by the network congestion precipitated by the CryptoKitties phenomenon in 2017, underscoring the imperative of addressing scalability challenges to accommodate burgeoning user bases and transaction volumes. While alternative cryptocurrencies such as EOS and Cardano offer potential remedies to scalability issues, the feasibility and efficacy of these solutions remain untested in real-world business environments. Moreover, the perceived value of BCT in tourism is contingent upon factors such as network size, miner incentives, and the consensus mechanism employed, whether proof of work (POW) and/or proof of share (POS) (Lewis et al., 2017). Consequently, the deployment of decentralized applications (DApps) in the tourism sector necessitates meticulous consideration of these multifaceted challenges, notwithstanding the manifold advantages offered by BCT.

BCT necessitates substantial user involvement, demanding a thorough understanding of fundamental concepts such as private keys, public keys, and digital wallet management (Maythu, Kwok, and Pei-Lee, 2024). As businesses transition from Web 2.0 to Web 3.0, significant operational transformations ensue, with user input assuming paramount importance in consumer-to-business interactions. Thus, companies embarking on blockchain adoption journeys must discern the most fitting blockchain types to align with their organizational needs, as the selection of an inappropriate blockchain type can detrimentally affect customer relationships and financial outcomes.

However, despite the potential benefits, the adoption of BCT in the tourism and hospitality sector faces notable impediments, prominently the lack of access to requisite technological infrastructure (Filimonau and Naumova, 2020; Sharma et al., 2021). This challenge encompasses the absence of essential infrastructure, technical expertise, and resources necessary for the successful implementation of BCT. Consequently, organizations may encounter difficulties in adopting BCT due to the associated costs and the steep learning curve involved (Mougayar, 2016; Toufaily et al., 2021).

Given the hospitality industry's emphasis on efficiency and speed, questions arise regarding the immediate suitability of BCT to meet the sector's needs, particularly in light of its constrained marketplace dynamics (Hua et al., 2019). Thus, the adoption of BCT in hospitality operations may be hindered by the inherent delays in transaction authorization processes (Stein et al., 2018). These delays, stemming from the security measures inherent in BCT, can result in prolonged

Future trends and challenges 103

waiting periods for transaction approval, potentially undermining the cost advantages typically associated with e-commerce transactions.

Additionally, network latency, defined as delays in data transmission between network points, presents another obstacle (Kizildag et al., 2019; Gillis, 2023). Network latency, caused by limited bandwidth, congestion, and security measures, impacts transaction speed and efficiency in blockchain networks (Sharma et al., 2021). In the tourism and hospitality sector, network latency can lead to delays in processing transactions, such as customer payments, affecting overall customer experience and satisfaction. Consequently, addressing network latency is crucial for overcoming scalability concerns and enhancing the adoption of BCT in the tourism sector (Sharma et al., 2021).

Moreover, the lack of interoperability in BCT poses a significant hurdle (Wegner, 1996). Interoperability, crucial for seamless data exchange between different systems, is challenging to achieve in blockchain due to the absence of standardization. The use of diverse protocols, consensus mechanisms, and data structures across blockchain platforms complicates collaboration and data exchange (Belchior et al., 2021; Lohachab, 2021). This lack of interoperability may lead to data isolation and inefficiencies, hindering the integration of BCT in the tourism and hospitality industry (Dutta et al., 2020; Erol et al., 2022).

Yet, the drawbacks linked to integrating BCT in the tourism sector also center on the complexities of cryptocurrency payments, especially vulnerability to hacker attacks. For instance, in 2018, a distributed denial of service (DDS) attack targeted a network of second-level payment channels for the Bitcoin Lightning Network blockchain, resulting in the disabling of 200 nodes, constituting 20% of the network (Panina et al., 2022).

Moreover, vulnerabilities such as the "Sybil attack," wherein a hacker assigns multiple identifiers to a single node, can disrupt network operations by exploiting temporary networks like Bitcoin and Ethereum (Panina et al., 2022). These vulnerabilities heighten the risk of encountering fraudulent transactions, as illustrated by scenarios wherein users exploit loopholes to facilitate fraudulent activities.

Furthermore, the "Eclipse attack" poses significant threats to blockchain systems by manipulating temporary networks to gain control over node access, enabling malicious actors to dominate consensus blocks. Compounding these concerns are technical challenges, such as potential failures in data loading, processing, and transmission due to the vast database size inherent in BCT (Nikitina and Tishchenko, 2018).

From another perspective, the adoption of BCT in the tourism and hospitality sector is impeded by market uncertainty, stemming from unpredictable and unstable market conditions (Sharma et al., 2021; Lubowiecki-Vikuk et al., 2023). This uncertainty manifests in various forms, including unclear regulatory frameworks, lack of standardization, and uncertain market demand, complicating decision-making processes for businesses considering investments in BCT (Sharma et al., 2021; Filimonau and Naumova, 2020; Kizildag et al., 2019).

Likewise, energy consumption emerges as a significant obstacle to the implementation of BCT (BCT) in the tourism and hospitality sector (Treiblmaier, 2022). The substantial energy usage associated with blockchain operations is widely acknowledged as a drawback to adopting blockchain-based solutions (Mucchi et al., 2022; Özgit and Adalıer, 2022). This is particularly evident in the case of Bitcoin, which consumes a considerable amount of energy due to the consensus protocols used to validate transactions and generate new blocks (De Vries and Stoll, 2021; Bada et al., 2021). The intensive computational processes involved in these protocols necessitate a significant electricity demand, posing challenges for companies seeking to justify the expenses associated with implementing BCT (Treiblmaier, 2022; Bada et al., 2021).

Along with that, companies embarking on in-house development of BCT encounter difficulties in sourcing skilled employees proficient in fundamental concepts such as private and public keys. This shortage underscores the heightened need for user involvement compared to conventional technologies, emphasizing the importance of recruiting and training personnel with a deep understanding of blockchain principles (Maythu, Kwok, and Pei-Lee, 2024).

Furthermore, the decentralization in the tourism sector threatens dominant players benefiting from existing structures, potentially weakening their influence. However, the prevalence of private blockchains among major players results in isolated networks, hindering comprehensive blockchain integration and impeding the emergence of new business models. Consequently, BCT has the capacity to challenge monopolies by decentralizing operations and eliminating intermediaries, thereby reshaping industry dynamics (Maythu, Kwok, and Pei-Lee, 2024).

Change management emerges as another formidable hurdle to widespread blockchain adoption, encompassing both internal organizational adjustments and broader industry-level transformations. Internally, businesses exhibit reluctance to enact organizational changes in the absence of significant operational challenges, particularly in the tourism sector where existing systems continue to function adequately. The disruptive potential of BCT to alter organizational hierarchies by fostering transparency and facilitating faster information exchange necessitates compelling incentives for enterprises to transition to blockchain (Maythu, Kwok, and Pei-Lee, 2024).

Legal challenges

A primary challenge is the lack of comprehensive regulations. BCT is relatively new, and many countries have yet to establish robust legal frameworks to govern its use, leading to uncertainties and risks. Issues such as data privacy and protection, governed by regulations like the General Data Protection Regulation (GDPR) in Europe, are particularly problematic for blockchain applications involving personal data storage and sharing.

The decentralized nature of BCT complicates regulatory oversight since it operates on a distributed network, making it difficult to determine jurisdiction and responsibility. This can hinder the enforcement of laws related to anti-money laundering (AML) and counter-terrorism financing (CTF). According to Wang et al. (2021), applying BCT without clear regulatory guidelines can lead to significant legal pitfalls. Regulatory uncertainty poses challenges for organizations looking to implement BCT solutions, as they must navigate complex legal and compliance requirements. Engaging with regulatory authorities, industry associations, and legal experts to stay informed about regulatory developments is crucial for mitigating risks and ensuring compliance with applicable laws.

Governments worldwide exhibit varying degrees of opposition to BCT, often due to concerns about losing control over financial and economic systems. Cryptocurrencies, a prominent application of BCT, can operate outside traditional financial regulatory frameworks, making it difficult for governments to monitor and control financial transactions. This loss of control can threaten monetary policies and financial stability. In response, some governments have imposed strict regulations or outright bans on certain blockchain activities. For instance, China has implemented extensive restrictions on cryptocurrency trading and mining activities, citing concerns about financial risk and fraud. Such government actions can stifle innovation and limit the potential benefits of BCT.

Pathan's research (2023) underscores the urgency of issuing laws to regulate cryptocurrencies, which have become potential alternative currencies. Even in countries where crypto is banned, digital cryptocurrency transactions for payments persist. Moreover, there is no international institution regulating cryptocurrency circulation, leading to inconsistencies where digital transactions are legal in one country but illegal in another. It is crucial for public institutions to adapt to these changes by involving government, private sector, and civil society.

BCT also raises national security concerns due to its potential use for illicit activities. The anonymity and decentralization provided by blockchain can be exploited for money laundering, terrorist financing, and other illegal activities. Governments fear that without proper oversight, BCT could become a tool for criminals to evade law enforcement.

Moreover, the security of blockchain networks themselves can be a national security issue. While blockchain is generally considered secure, vulnerabilities can still exist. Poorly designed smart contracts or consensus mechanisms can be exploited by malicious actors. The scalability issues of some blockchain networks can also lead to inefficiencies and vulnerabilities that could be targeted in cyberattacks. Dadkhah et al. (2022) highlighted that wherever human knowledge and interpretation are needed to resolve disputes, blockchain and smart contracts cannot be implemented and must be referred to a third party. This indicates that automated systems alone cannot address all legal and security issues, necessitating human oversight and intervention.

Despite blockchain's potential to foster decentralization and transparency, adherence to prevailing legal and regulatory frameworks is imperative. However, the regulatory landscape governing blockchain remains ambiguous and nascent in many jurisdictions, leading to uncertainty and hindrances in its implementation (Ahl et al., 2022). The absence of well-defined regulations and guidelines exacerbates uncertainty for businesses endeavoring to embrace BCT. Ambiguities within legal frameworks, particularly concerning data protection, intellectual property rights, and smart contracts, may serve as barriers to adoption as organizations grapple with understanding their legal obligations and potential liabilities (Choobineh et al., 2022). Thus, the adoption of blockchain necessitates navigating complex regulatory terrains, further complicating the integration process.

Adhering to AML and know-your-customer (KYC) regulations, alongside complying with data privacy laws, financial regulations, and industry-specific mandates, poses significant challenges. Achieving regulatory compliance requires considerable resources and commitment, particularly for organizations operating across multiple jurisdictions. The cross-border nature of blockchain networks adds another layer of complexity to regulatory compliance. Variations in legal frameworks and regulatory approaches to BCT among different countries can lead to conflicting regulations. Businesses engaged in international transactions or with global operations must adeptly navigate these complexities and ensure compliance with relevant regulations in each jurisdiction (Sun et al., 2021).

Santos and Duffy (2022) delve into two fundamental GDPR principles pertinent to blockchain technologies. The first principle stipulates that for each personal data point, there must be at least one natural or legal person, known as the data controller, to whom data subjects can address their rights under EU data protection law. These data controllers are obligated to adhere to the GDPR's requirements. However, concerning GDPR regulations, there is apprehension regarding blockchain's pursuit of decentralization, which may blur the definition of "controllership" and impede the assignment of responsibility and accountability (Han et al., 2020). The GDPR's second assumption revolves around the notion that data can be modified or erased as necessary to comply with legal requirements.

Assessing blockchain compliance with GDPR reveals fundamental conflicts, including the question of whether data on the public blockchain constitutes sensitive personal data (Han et al., 2020). If such data is categorized as personal data, adherence to GDPR regulations becomes imperative. Another contention revolves around whether data can be adequately anonymized to meet GDPR requirements (Han et al., 2020).

Beyond EU data protection regulations, the United States boasts several data protection laws, such as the California Consumer Privacy Act (CCPA) (Beleuz et al., 2022). Fedorova and Skobleva (2020) elucidated the complexities inherent in aligning blockchain with the CCPA. Analogous to the GDPR challenges, the distributed ledger and data immutability features of blockchain may clash with the

108 *The Future of Blockchain in Tourism and Hospitality*

obligations of the CCPA (Beleuz et al., 2022). Consequently, identifying and upholding responsible controllers within the blockchain realm becomes challenging.

Financial challenges

BCT (BCT) presents significant hurdles and obstacles to broader implementation due to regulatory ambiguity and uncertainty, particularly concerning budgetary and financial planning (Ivaninskiy and Ivashkovskaya, 2022). Organizational leaders, irrespective of their personal views on blockchain, must account for existing budgetary requirements and obligations. Deploying BCT necessitates both substantial initial capital investments and ongoing operational expenditures. In the absence of consistent, comprehensible, and enforceable regulatory policies—or at least the anticipation of such guidelines—blockchain projects and initiatives risk stagnation (Wilkie and Smith, 2021).

Furthermore, the economic challenges of adopting BCT relate to the high costs of acquiring and implementing the technology, which includes technical capabilities and personnel training for blockchain system operations. These costs can significantly impede the widespread adoption of innovative practices among travel companies (Panina et al., 2022). Since blockchain is a feature-dependent technology, the final cost varies depending on the project requirements. Generally, substantial capital expenditure is required to implement the necessary blockchain infrastructure initially, which may ultimately affect financial sustainability (Thakur et al., 2019; Lohmer and Lasch, 2020; Lin and Liao, 2017; Azati Team, 2021).

In the tourism and hospitality sector, BCT faces challenges within the industry due to its associated costs and the learning curve involved (Mougayar, 2016; Toufaily et al., 2021). Operational costs further complicate the adoption of blockchain in the hospitality industry. Running Bitcoin, for example, is currently unprofitable for small-scale businesses, which are predominant in the hospitality sector (UNWTO, 2019). Additionally, BCT often entails lengthy waiting periods for transaction authorization, potentially eroding cost advantages and hindering efficiency (Stein et al., 2018).

Despite these economic challenges, the risk posed by cost implications can be managed by system developers through equitable cost distribution among end users and operators. Designing BCT

Future trends and challenges 109

as multi-chains accommodating different currencies can mitigate the risk of survival between dominant and new coins (Nam et al., 2022). Although increased costs are a potential risk, it is essential to propose solutions to address them to ensure the financial sustainability of blockchain projects.

The establishment and maintenance of blockchain infrastructure entail considerable expenses, covering costs for hardware, software, network infrastructure, and data storage (Li et al., 2019). Moreover, the energy-intensive nature of blockchain mining operations can exacerbate operational expenditures, adding to the overall cost burden of blockchain implementation.

In addition to infrastructure costs, the adoption of BCT entails the need for proficient developers and technical expertise, which can contribute to elevated development expenditures compared to conventional software solutions (Islam et al., 2021). Businesses venturing into blockchain implementation may face supplementary costs associated with employee training and the adaptation of organizational practices to accommodate the new technology.

Scalability emerges as another prominent cost-related challenge in blockchain adoption (Andoni et al., 2019). As blockchain networks undergo expansion and witness heightened usage, the expenses linked to processing and validating transactions may surge. Addressing scalability issues and augmenting network capacity to accommodate a burgeoning transaction volume often necessitates substantial financial investments in infrastructure enhancements and optimization, thereby further amplifying the overall expenditure.

Furthermore, the sustained operation of blockchain networks requires continual maintenance efforts, robust security protocols, and regular updates to ensure their functionality and integrity (Li et al., 2021). The associated expenses for monitoring, addressing vulnerabilities, and implementing necessary updates play a pivotal role in upholding the security and reliability of the blockchain ecosystem (Srivastava et al., 2020). Thus, companies embarking on blockchain adoption must allocate resources toward troubleshooting network issues, resolving conflicts, and fulfilling governance obligations.

The substantial costs and endeavors associated with ensuring regulatory adherence, particularly for organizations with multinational operations, can be daunting (Sun et al., 2021). The cross-border nature of blockchain networks exacerbates regulatory compliance complexities, with differing legal frameworks across jurisdictions compounding the challenge. Organizations engaging in international transactions or maintaining a global presence must adeptly navigate these intricacies to ensure compliance with the diverse regulatory landscapes in each jurisdiction they operate within.

The challenges associated with costs in BCT are intricately linked to its energy consumption. For example, a single Bitcoin transaction consumes approximately 160 kWh of electricity (Grech and Camilleri, 2017), which not only contributes to high operational costs but also underscores the environmental impact of blockchain operations. The need for efficient data storage further complicates this issue, as redundant data storage practices increase energy demands and operational expenses. Therefore, managing energy use effectively is crucial for mitigating the overall costs and environmental footprint of blockchain technologies.

Moreover, the transition from a centralized to a decentralized framework entails its own set of expenditures, including those related to the procurement of new hardware and software resources (Arndt and Guercio, 2020). Therefore, there is a need to allocate resources for educating and training personnel across various departments, extending beyond the IT team, to ensure widespread awareness and comprehension of BCT (Zheng et al., 2017).

Social challenges

The lack of awareness and understanding about blockchain may hinder its implementation and assimilation across diverse sectors. Despite the familiarity with cryptocurrencies such as Bitcoin, Ethereum, Litecoin, Monero, among others, many individuals may not fully comprehend the underlying technology or its broader scope beyond financial transactions. Rugeviciute and Mehrpouya (2019) observed a lack of awareness among clients regarding blockchain and its applications. Educating stakeholders about the advantages of BCT and its implications for data ownership, accessibility, and privacy becomes imperative. This educational endeavor can aid enterprises in bolstering their adoption rates of blockchain, thereby fostering customer acceptance of the technology.

In terms of awareness, there exists divergence among experts' perceptions of the current scenario. While all acknowledge an increase in awareness, particularly in recent years, some experts maintain that awareness remains critical. Others argue that awareness has reached

Future trends and challenges 111

a sufficient level, albeit the need to define significant use cases at the strategic management level persists (Amsyar et al., 2020). Large corporations are leading the way in adopting BCT by creating specialized divisions to implement blockchain applications. These companies are driving digital transformation initiatives across various industries. In contrast, many small- and medium-sized enterprises have not yet embraced BCT, with several IT executives failing to recognize its potential. This divide in perception appears in two main ways: some managers are unaware of possible uses and efficiency improvements within their industries, while others see blockchain as a universal solution to all challenges. Particularly with smart contracts, there is a widespread belief that these contracts can significantly improve every process. However, there has been a gradual shift from viewing blockchain solely as a tool to recognizing its broader potential. Nonetheless, companies lacking deep knowledge of blockchain should strive to better understand its basic concepts and benefits. Specifically, further research and development are needed to explore the advantages of creating collaborative production networks through BCT, enabling decentralized networks across different companies without centralized control.

There is a noticeable gap in knowledge acquisition between large enterprises and small- and medium-sized enterprises (SMEs). While larger companies have invested significantly in training their current workforce, hiring specialists, and even establishing dedicated blockchain departments, SMEs have not kept pace. Adding to this challenge is the shortage of skilled workers, especially developers, which experts unanimously recognize. However, the consulting market is well-positioned to help SMEs in the initial stages of building competency (Lohmer and Lasch, 2020).

Overall, the challenges outlined by these authors can be categorized into four principal categories (Table 5.2): societal, technical, financial, and legal, based on their respective descriptions and characteristics (Dadkhah, Rahimnia, and Filimonau, 2022).

Recommendations and considerations for stakeholders and policymakers regarding blockchain in tourism

The integration of BCT in the tourism sector presents both significant opportunities and challenges. For stakeholders and policymakers to harness the full potential of blockchain, they must address various

Table 5.2 BCT challenges

Challenges	Definition	Components
Technical	The BCT technology is not mature yet, so there will be challenges for its use. There are also concerns about required infrastructure. It highlights security and privacy concerns regarding the current version of the BCT. Different studies indicate that there are some security flaws in current BCT.	Scalability issues Energy consumption Privacy Internet access Security Requires desired level of readiness Immature cryptocurrencies Blockchain overhead Limited number of experts
Social	Challenges that arise due to tourists' interaction with technology such as lack of knowledge and resistance.	Lack of awareness Education and training
Financial	The BCT can pose many costs to societies for its adoption.	Cost
Legal	Legislation and political decisions can be a challenge for the BCT usage, because governments will have less control on cryptocurrencies.	Regulatory issues Government opposition National security

Source: Own elaboration based on Dadkhah et al. (2022).

concerns and obstacles related to stakeholder consensus, competitive dynamics, financial transparency, data security, and regulatory frameworks. The following recommendations and considerations, drawn from existing literature, provide a comprehensive overview of the necessary steps for successful blockchain adoption in tourism.

Tham and Sigala (2020) suggests that achieving consensus among stakeholders to leverage blockchain for mutual benefits is challenging, particularly in the hyper-competitive tourism sector where the demand for financial transparency may deter participation due to competitive concerns. Many tourism businesses, as noted by Ehret and Wirtz (2017), prioritize brand goodwill and consistent service excellence, making them hesitant to adopt transparent blockchain practices. Effective blockchain participation requires equitable contributions from all stakeholders as value drivers within the ecosystem. Therefore,

Future trends and challenges   113

enhancing data security awareness and establishing robust regulatory frameworks are crucial for blockchain's successful implementation in tourism. Thus, stakeholders and policymakers must prioritize achieving consensus among them, enhancing data security awareness, offering training on innovative technologies, and developing comprehensive regulatory frameworks to effectively integrate BCT into the tourism sector.

Based on the work of Widhiasthini et al. (2024), a set of recommendations and considerations are outlined below. These steps will not only address current challenges but also enable regions and businesses to capitalize on the competitive advantages provided by blockchain.

Legal recognition of blockchain elements

Developing legal frameworks to recognize blockchain-based elements such as signatures, timestamps, validations, and documents is crucial for integrating blockchain into the legal system. This means that laws and regulations need to be updated or created to specifically acknowledge the validity and enforceability of these digital elements. For instance, just as traditional handwritten signatures are legally binding, digital signatures created through BCT must also be recognized. Timestamps and validations on blockchain should be legally accepted as proof of the timing and authenticity of transactions and documents. Policymakers must ensure these digital elements meet certain standards for security, reliability, and integrity to prevent fraud and misuse. This will involve close collaboration between legislators, legal experts, and technologists to ensure the new regulations are both legally sound and technically feasible.

Standards and certifications

To ensure BCT's reliability and security, establishing standards and certification processes is essential. Standards will provide a consistent framework for how blockchain systems should operate, ensuring they meet specific security, performance, and interoperability criteria. Certification processes will help verify that blockchain applications comply with these standards, building trust among users and regulators. These standards can be developed in collaboration with international bodies like the International Organization for Standardization (ISO)

114   *The Future of Blockchain in Tourism and Hospitality*

and industry groups. Certification can be managed by accredited organizations that rigorously test blockchain systems. This approach not only enhances the technology's credibility but also provides a clear guideline for developers to follow, ensuring their solutions are robust and compliant with regulatory requirements.

Education and training

Educating legal professionals, regulators, and other stakeholders about BCT is crucial for its successful integration into the legal framework. Many in the legal field may not fully understand how blockchain works or its potential legal implications. Training programs, workshops, and continuous professional development courses can help bridge this knowledge gap. These educational initiatives should cover the technical aspects of blockchain, its benefits, and potential legal issues, such as data privacy and security concerns. By enhancing the understanding of BCT among legal professionals and regulators, they can more effectively draft, interpret, and enforce new regulations, ensuring blockchain's legal recognition is both practical and beneficial.

Cross-jurisdictional harmonization

Cross-jurisdictional harmonization of legal and regulatory frameworks is essential for BCT, which often operates across borders. Different countries have varying laws and regulations, which can create complex challenges for blockchain applications that span multiple jurisdictions. Harmonization efforts involve coordinating with international regulatory bodies to develop a unified legal approach to blockchain. This can include creating international treaties or agreements that set out common standards and principles. Harmonizing regulations helps prevent legal conflicts, reduce regulatory arbitrage, and foster a more predictable legal environment for blockchain businesses. Effective harmonization also involves recognizing the need for local adaptations while maintaining core principles that ensure consistency and interoperability across borders.

Frameworks for cooperation

Establishing frameworks for cooperation among regulators and legislators is critical to managing cross-jurisdictional issues in BCT.

Future trends and challenges 115

These frameworks can take the form of bilateral or multilateral agreements that facilitate information sharing, joint investigations, and coordinated regulatory actions. Cooperation mechanisms might include regular meetings, shared databases, and collaborative research initiatives. Such frameworks help address issues like market manipulation, fraud, and monopolies that can arise in the global blockchain landscape. They also enable regulators to collectively respond to emerging threats and challenges, ensuring a cohesive and effective regulatory approach that supports innovation while protecting consumers and maintaining market integrity.

Common standards

Developing common standards for BCT is vital to ensure consistency and interoperability across different jurisdictions. Common standards provide a baseline for what is considered secure, reliable, and legally compliant in blockchain systems. These standards can cover various aspects, such as data security, transaction integrity, and interoperability protocols. By adopting internationally recognized standards, countries can facilitate cross-border blockchain transactions and collaborations, reducing legal and technical barriers. Common standards also help build trust among users, investors, and regulators, as they provide assurance that blockchain applications meet certain quality and security benchmarks. This promotes broader acceptance and adoption of BCT in various sectors.

Regulatory clarity

Providing clear guidelines on the legal status and enforceability of blockchain transactions is essential to ensure that users and businesses understand their rights and obligations. BCT often involves pseudonymous or anonymous transactions, which can complicate legal enforcement. Clear regulatory guidelines can specify under what conditions blockchain transactions are legally binding and enforceable, addressing concerns related to pseudonymity and anonymity. These guidelines should also outline the procedures for resolving disputes and enforcing legal judgments in the context of blockchain. By offering regulatory clarity, policymakers can reduce uncertainty, prevent misuse of the technology, and foster a legal environment that supports legitimate blockchain applications.

116 *The Future of Blockchain in Tourism and Hospitality*

Law enforcement training

Training law enforcement agencies to handle blockchain-related cases is crucial for effectively addressing criminal activities that exploit the technology. Blockchain's pseudonymity can make it challenging for law enforcement to track and prosecute offenders. Specialized training programs can equip law enforcement personnel with the knowledge and tools needed to investigate blockchain transactions, identify suspects, and gather admissible evidence. This training should cover blockchain basics, advanced forensic techniques, and the legal framework governing digital transactions. Enhanced law enforcement capabilities can deter criminal activities on blockchain networks and ensure that perpetrators are brought to justice, thereby maintaining public trust in the technology.

Technological solutions

Encouraging the development and adoption of technological solutions to enhance transparency and traceability in blockchain transactions can help address enforcement challenges. Solutions such as identity verification mechanisms, zero-knowledge proofs, and advanced cryptographic techniques can strike a balance between maintaining user privacy and ensuring legal compliance. These technologies can enable the identification of transaction participants when necessary for legal purposes, without compromising the fundamental benefits of blockchain, such as decentralization and security. Policymakers should support research and innovation in this area, potentially through funding initiatives or regulatory sandboxes that allow for the testing of new solutions in a controlled environment.

Define roles and responsibilities

Clearly defining the roles and responsibilities of various actors within blockchain networks is essential for establishing accountability. Blockchain ecosystems often involve multiple stakeholders, including developers, validators, miners, and end-users, each with different levels of control and influence. By delineating the specific duties and obligations of these actors, regulations can ensure that each party understands their potential liabilities and responsibilities. This clarity helps in assigning blame and enforcing accountability when issues

Future trends and challenges 117

arise, such as security breaches or fraudulent activities. Policymakers should engage with industry experts and stakeholders to develop comprehensive definitions that reflect the realities of blockchain operations.

Liability frameworks

Developing liability frameworks that specify the conditions under which different actors in blockchain networks can be held accountable is crucial for addressing accountability issues. These frameworks should consider the varying degrees of control and influence each actor has over the network. For example, core developers who design and maintain the blockchain protocol might bear more responsibility for systemic issues than individual users. The frameworks should outline the legal recourse available to affected parties and the penalties for non-compliance. By providing a clear and equitable approach to liability, these frameworks can encourage responsible behavior and reduce the risk of legal disputes within the blockchain ecosystem.

Enforcement mechanisms

Creating practical and efficient mechanisms for identifying and holding accountable the responsible parties in blockchain networks is necessary for effective enforcement. Blockchain's decentralized nature can make it difficult to pinpoint the individuals or entities responsible for specific actions. Enforcement mechanisms might include advanced tracking and analysis tools, cooperation with blockchain developers to implement accountability features, and international collaboration to address cross-border cases. These mechanisms should be designed to operate within existing legal frameworks while accommodating the unique characteristics of BCT. Effective enforcement not only enhances accountability but also builds trust in blockchain systems, encouraging wider adoption and innovation.

Adapt GDPR for blockchain

Updating the GDPR to address the unique characteristics of BCT is essential for ensuring data protection compliance. The GDPR, designed for centralized data processing systems, poses challenges for blockchain's decentralized nature. Policymakers need to adapt GDPR provisions to account for features like immutability and distributed

118 *The Future of Blockchain in Tourism and Hospitality*

storage. This might involve clarifying how rights like data erasure (the "right to be forgotten") and data access can be exercised on blockchain platforms. Adaptations could also include guidelines for pseudonymization techniques and data minimization practices that align with blockchain's architecture. By making these adjustments, regulators can ensure that blockchain applications comply with data protection laws while preserving their operational advantages.

Privacy-enhancing technologies

Promoting the use of privacy-enhancing technologies (PETs) within blockchain systems can help achieve compliance with data protection regulations. PETs such as zero-knowledge proofs, homomorphic encryption, and secure multi-party computation allow for secure data processing without exposing sensitive information. Encouraging the adoption of these technologies can help blockchain developers design systems that protect user privacy while meeting legal requirements. Policymakers can support this by funding research into PETs, creating incentives for their implementation, and incorporating PET guidelines into regulatory frameworks. By leveraging PETs, blockchain applications can offer robust privacy protections, fostering trust and compliance in sensitive sectors like finance and healthcare.

Clear guidance

Providing clear guidance on how blockchain applications can comply with GDPR is critical for ensuring that developers and businesses understand their legal obligations. This guidance should outline best practices for integrating data protection principles into blockchain systems, such as data minimization, encryption, and pseudonymization. It should also address specific blockchain features, such as immutable ledgers and decentralized storage, offering practical solutions for compliance. Regulators can issue detailed guidelines, conduct workshops, and develop toolkits to assist blockchain projects in navigating data protection requirements. Clear guidance helps demystify the regulatory landscape, enabling innovation while safeguarding individual privacy rights.

Case-by-case assessment

Developing frameworks for assessing competition issues in blockchain applications on a case-by-case basis is essential due to the technology's

Future trends and challenges 119

diverse use cases and market dynamics. Unlike traditional industries, where competition issues can often be assessed using established metrics and criteria, the blockchain space is characterized by a wide variety of platforms, protocols, and use cases. Each blockchain project can vary significantly in terms of its architecture, governance, user base, and market impact. Therefore, a one-size-fits-all approach to competition policy would likely be ineffective and could stifle innovation. A case-by-case assessment allows regulators to consider the specific circumstances and nuances of each blockchain application. For instance, a public blockchain used for decentralized finance (DeFi) may present different competition concerns compared to a private blockchain used for supply chain management. Factors such as the degree of decentralization, the role of intermediaries, market share, and potential network effects need to be carefully evaluated. In this regard, by adopting a case-by-case approach, regulators can tailor their assessments to the unique attributes of each blockchain application. This flexibility ensures that competition policies are fair, effective, and supportive of innovation. Policymakers should also engage with industry experts, blockchain developers, and other stakeholders to gather insights and refine their assessment frameworks. Continuous dialogue and collaboration with the blockchain community can help regulators stay informed about technological advancements and emerging trends, enabling them to address competition issues proactively and effectively.

Thus, given the complexities and the socio-technical nature of blockchain systems, practical suggestions for government policies are essential for fostering a conductive environment for blockchain development. Therefore, governments should focus on fostering social innovation and creating a robust blockchain ecosystem. This involves encouraging the use of blockchain beyond specific domains like cryptocurrencies to wider societal benefits, such as enhancing public services, improving transparency in governance, and fostering community engagement. Policies should promote the integration of BCT into various sectors through pilot projects and public–private partnerships. Blockchain development should not be a one-off initiative but a continuous process involving all stakeholders. Governments need to engage with industry experts, academics, civil society, and the public to create inclusive policies that reflect diverse perspectives and needs. This participatory approach ensures that blockchain solutions are sustainable and aligned with societal values and expectations.

6 Regulatory environment and ethical considerations

Data privacy and security concerns

The emergence of new technologies often prompts a reevaluation of fundamental social concepts, such as trust. Indeed, the acceptance and adoption rate of an emerging technology are significantly influenced by its level of understanding and trustworthiness. In the case of blockchain technology, adopters may experience feelings of uncertainty or skepticism when confronted with a novel system that necessitates a reimagining of traditional approaches to data management and sharing within societies. This challenge is particularly pronounced for blockchains, where trust serves as a pivotal force driving development.

Paradoxically, trust assumes a dual role in the context of blockchains. At its core, trust is the foundational concept upon which blockchain technology is constructed, and as such, it should inspire confidence and trust among its users. Previous studies have highlighted that trust-related concerns pose significant obstacles to the advancement of blockchain initiatives within firms (Shin, 2019; Kshetri, 2018). Numerous cases examined in these studies illustrate that while blockchain technology was designed to address issues of trust, it is, in turn, hindered by trust-related challenges, thereby impeding its adoption and diffusion (Kshetri, 2018). This suggests that resolving trust-related issues is imperative for the development of blockchain technology within a socio-technical framework.

In addition to trust, usability and user acceptance represent significant hurdles for blockchain technology. Despite its potential, many blockchain systems are developed by technically proficient individuals, resulting in interfaces that often lack user-friendliness

DOI: 10.4324/9781003521617-7

Regulatory environment and ethical considerations   121

and intuitive design. In regions where blockchain awareness and understanding remain limited, these usability issues can impede widespread adoption (Lapointe and Fishbane, 2019).

Exclusion within blockchain systems can occur both at the organizational and individual levels. Organizations governing these systems may monopolize networks, controlling participation and posing challenges for excluded stakeholders to engage in transactions (Fischer, 2018; Palas and Bunduchi, 2020). Meanwhile, individual users may face unintentional exclusion due to factors such as computational literacy and limited access to necessary hardware (Lapointe and Fishbane, 2019). A socio-technical approach is necessary to address and remedy these usability challenges, ensuring that blockchain technology can achieve its full potential and gain broader acceptance.

In the realm of technology, it is emphasized that digital systems must prioritize safety and operate in full accordance with individuals' fundamental rights (European Commission, 2022). Online platforms should be secured and shielded against misinformation, while also demonstrating resilience against cybercrime, encompassing data breaches and cyberattacks. This entails safeguarding digital identities from theft or manipulation (European Commission, 2022).

Security within the context of blockchain technology encompasses protection against both physical and non-physical harm, whether perpetrated by humans or otherwise. One of the primary issues with blockchain security is its susceptibility to fraud and hacking, which has been evidenced in numerous instances globally (Smith and Johnson, 2021). The transparency and decentralization that are the hallmarks of blockchain can paradoxically make it a target for malicious activities (Garcia et al., 2020). For example, pyramid schemes that promise distributorship or franchise opportunities have exploited blockchain's open nature, leading to significant financial losses for individuals. A notable security breach occurred in 2016 when major credit card firms experienced a massive theft of customer data. This incident compromised 75 million credit cards (Krishna, 2021). The breach underscored the vulnerability of digital data and highlighted the shortcomings in security measures implemented by these firms.

Indeed, blockchain technology is heralded for its robust security features, largely due to the hashing algorithms and sophisticated encryption embedded within its system architecture (Yang, 2019). These measures theoretically ensure a high level of security, making blockchain an attractive option for various applications. However,

122 The Future of Blockchain in Tourism and Hospitality

despite these sophisticated security mechanisms, blockchain security remains a significant concern. The open-source nature of blockchain networks exacerbates these vulnerabilities, as seen in multiple high-profile incidents (Joshi et al., 2018; Shin, 2019).

Privacy, often regarded as a cornerstone of blockchain technology, also represents a significant concern. Blockchain's design inherently imposes limitations on privacy. The distributed nature of blockchain means that every full node processing transaction has access to transaction data, making it publicly available and traceable back to its origin (Bancroft and Reid, 2017). This is particularly problematic in jurisdictions with stringent privacy regulations, such as Korea's Personal Information Protection Act, which mirrors the General Data Protection Regulation (GDPR) of Europe. These regulations aim to safeguard individuals' privacy rights and prevent the abuse, leakage, or misuse of personal data.

Privacy is a critical issue in blockchain technology, particularly in the context of centralized data storage and potential unauthorized access (Zwitter, 2014). The security of raw data is essential for maintaining user privacy within blockchain systems (Kshetri, 2018). Blockchain protects user identities through e-wallet providers, yet if these providers are compromised, user identities can be exposed, as blockchain is not fully anonymous. Controlled data sharing, such as releasing transaction abstracts while keeping original data in traditional databases, can enhance privacy. However, blockchain's requirement for indefinite data sharing and permanent storage poses challenges, including potential violations of the right to be forgotten. Innovative privacy mechanisms and flexible data-sharing policies are necessary to balance transaction facilitation with privacy protection.

Within blockchain systems, two distinct privacy concerns are prone to emerge. The first concern pertains to rectifying inaccuracies in personal data. Given the immutable nature of blockchain ledgers, it is imperative that no personal or sensitive information is directly stored on the ledger. The second privacy issue revolves around data dissemination. Since the ledger is distributed across all nodes within a network, it is crucial that only data appropriate for network-wide distribution is stored on the network. To address these privacy concerns, enhancing transparency within systems becomes essential. Transparency within systems encompasses public institutions, private online services, and algorithmic operations.

Regulatory environment and ethical considerations 123

According to the European Union (2022), people have the right to be informed when engaging with AI and algorithms. The transparency of pertinent information plays a crucial role in ensuring accountability, safety, provision of public services, and obtaining informed consent (Turilli and Floridi, 2009). However, it is essential to carefully consider the context before disclosing sensitive data to mitigate ethical concerns. This principle is particularly relevant to data stored within blockchain systems, given the immutability of the ledger. Nevertheless, this same attribute can be leveraged to enhance transparency, especially within public institutions and governmental processes.

Ethical and social implications

Ethical considerations and regulatory compliance are crucial in blockchain adoption. Governments should establish clear guidelines and frameworks to protect user rights, ensure data privacy, and prevent misuse of blockchain technology. This includes developing standards for data protection, implementing robust auditing mechanisms, and fostering an ethical culture among blockchain developers and users (Tang et al., 2019).

Within the sphere of blockchain technology, the concept of respecting human dignity involves ethical considerations regarding the requirements of blockchain system users and the repercussions of these systems. It is paramount that autonomous entities, such as smart contracts, do not surpass human agents in authority, as this poses a risk of dehumanizing individuals in their interactions with the technology, thereby infringing upon their inherent human dignity (European Commission, 2022). However, it is noteworthy that blockchain technology can also serve to advance certain objectives outlined by the European Union, such as safeguarding "the right to freedom of expression in the online environment, without fear of being censored or intimidated" (European Commission, 2022, p. 5).

Given the rapid pace of technological change, ensuring the longevity of blockchain platforms is an ethical concern. This includes planning for future upgrades and the possibility of migrating to new platforms without loss of data integrity or functionality. By examining these facets through the lens of ethical deployment, stakeholders can navigate the complex interplay between innovation and responsibility. For example, a blockchain-based supply chain solution should

124　*The Future of Blockchain in Tourism and Hospitality*

enhance transparency without compromising trade secrets, while being accessible to various participants in the ecosystem, from multinational corporations to local farmers (Lu and Xu, 2017; Tian, 2016, 2017). Similarly, a cryptocurrency platform should prioritize energy-efficient algorithms to align with environmental sustainability goals. The ethical deployment of blockchain technology demands a multifaceted approach that considers long-term implications for society at large.

Furthermore, security is paramount for blockchain networks, as vulnerabilities can lead to significant financial and reputational damage. Ethical considerations include the robustness of cryptographic methods and the responsibility to update and patch systems as new threats emerge. The energy consumption of blockchain, particularly proof-of-work systems, has raised environmental concerns, making it essential to choose or develop more sustainable consensus mechanisms and consider the carbon footprint of blockchain operations (Baruffaldi and Sternberg, 2018; Korpela et al., 2017; Kshetri, 2018).

Navigating the complex landscape of international regulations poses a challenge. Ethical blockchain deployment requires adherence to laws while advocating for regulatory frameworks that recognize the unique aspects of blockchain technology. The introduction of blockchain systems can disrupt existing markets and labor forces, necessitating consideration of socio-economic consequences and support for transitions for those affected (Treiblmaier et al.,2020).

Moreover, in blockchain implementation, decentralized authentication of transaction records and data storage ensures equal participation among all constituents, enhancing system failure tolerance and attack resistance. The interconnection of multiple services, like cloud computing, further bolsters this resilience. These features enable blockchain to address moral dilemmas caused by unreliable data sources, improving decision-making capabilities.

Blockchain systems often outperform traditional centralized systems. However, challenges arise in development equality. Despite open-sourced protocols and software, core platform contributions are limited to a small group of programmers, raising concerns about developer diversity and technocratic control (Filippi and Loveluck, 2016). As most developers focus on application-level development, maintaining blockchain's neutrality for the entire ecosystem, rather than specific business interests, is crucial.

Regulatory environment and ethical considerations 125

Sustainable and diverse blockchain communities are necessary for continuous technological improvements. The survival of the fittest principle can help eliminate inactive applications and promote fair support for all upper level applications. Data accessibility in blockchain technology is ensured by the distributed computing mechanism rather than by any single party, eliminating the need for complex data policies (Yaga et al., 2019; Mohan, 2018). Accessible technology varies with the permission model: permissioned (private) blockchains restrict access within an organization for maximum security, while permissionless (public) blockchains, such as cryptocurrencies, are entirely open. Consortium blockchains offer a middle ground, providing access to internal and selected external parties.

Blockchain's inherent traceability ensures that all activities are recorded, addressing moral responsibility issues and aiding in the prevention of abuses and crimes (Mittelstadt et al., 2016; Johnson et al., 2015). For instance, Bitcoin records have been instrumental in uncovering human traffickers (Portnoff et al., 2017).

Blockchain's regulatory framework in the tourism and hospitality sector

The integration of blockchain technology in the tourism and hospitality industries is still in its early stages, with the regulatory framework governing its use continually evolving. Governments and regulatory bodies worldwide are working to develop guidelines and regulations to ensure the safe and effective use of blockchain, while also protecting consumers and businesses.

Consumer protection is paramount in blockchain applications within tourism. Ensuring transparent pricing, secure transactions, and mechanisms for dispute resolution is crucial. Blockchain's immutable ledger enhances consumer protection by providing an unalterable record of transactions, aiding in dispute resolution, and ensuring accountability (European Commission, 2023).

Standardization and interoperability are essential for effective blockchain adoption. Regulatory bodies are focusing on developing standards to ensure seamless integration and communication between different blockchain systems (European Commission, 2023). Compliance with existing laws, particularly anti-money laundering (AML) and know-your-customer (KYC) regulations, is critical for blockchain applications in tourism, where financial transactions are

126 *The Future of Blockchain in Tourism and Hospitality*

frequent and often cross-border. The Financial Action Task Force (FATF) has issued guidelines to ensure blockchain compliance with AML and KYC requirements (Grzyb (2023).

International collaborations are crucial for developing a cohesive regulatory framework. Organizations like the International Air Transport Association (IATA) and the World Travel and Tourism Council (WTTC) are working with blockchain developers and regulatory bodies to create guidelines that facilitate blockchain adoption in tourism while maintaining regulatory compliance (IATA, 2018.

Thus, the integration of blockchain technology in tourism and hospitality presents significant opportunities but also requires a robust regulatory framework to protect consumers and ensure compliance with existing laws. Ongoing efforts by regulatory bodies and international collaborations are essential to developing standards and guidelines that will enable the safe and effective use of blockchain in these industries.

Data privacy and security concerns

In the tourism and hospitality sector, vast amounts of personal data are collected, including travel itineraries, payment information, and personal preferences. Blockchain technology can enhance data security through its decentralized and immutable nature. However, this also raises significant concerns regarding data privacy and compliance with regulations like the GDPR. The immutable nature of blockchain ensures that once data is recorded, it cannot be altered. While this provides security, it also means that personal data cannot be easily deleted, posing challenges for compliance with GDPR's "right to be forgotten" (Calvaresi et al., 2019).

Smart contracts can automate and secure bookings, payments, and other transactions in the tourism sector. Ensuring the security of these transactions is critical to gaining consumer trust and promoting widespread adoption (Yang, 2019). Therefore, blockchain technology offers significant benefits for data security in the tourism and hospitality sector. However, addressing concerns related to data privacy, regulatory compliance, and future risks such as quantum computing is essential.

Ethical and social implications

Destinations with limited resources often grapple with high corruption levels, necessitating the establishment of reliable systems. A notable

Regulatory environment and ethical considerations 127

example is Moldova, where, according to Ozdemir et al., (2020), blockchain (BC) technology can combat corruption and increase citizens' incomes by decentralizing and removing industry boundaries. Similarly, Tham and Sigala (2020) highlight that BC fosters equal opportunities within the tourism industry, creating an inclusive business environment instead of a fragmented ecosystem. Banerji (2022) emphasize that BC's decentralization and immutable digital-asset history reduce fraud risk. Additionally, Dudin and Kononova (2020) illustrate through the Russian Federation's tourism sector that governmental intervention and BC usage are vital for development, as relying solely on recreational resources does not guarantee success. BC's transparency aids regional and national economic growth by promoting local agrotourism, ensuring product traceability due to its distributed nature. This is particularly beneficial for wine and food tourism, where certifying local food and beverages' quality, provenance, history, and traditions attracts tourists. Supporting this, Baralla et al. (2019) propose a BC-based system with smart contracts for transparent, reliable product tracking. Tested with Sardinian local food, this model demonstrated effective information sharing, allowing customers to access detailed product information and verify its provenance and characteristics.

Blockchain technology has the potential to democratize access to travel services by reducing the power of intermediaries and allowing for more direct transactions between service providers and consumers. This can lead to lower costs and increased access to travel opportunities for a broader range of people. By lowering transaction costs and simplifying processes, blockchain can make travel more accessible to individuals from diverse socio-economic backgrounds (Dierksmeier and Seele, 2020).

Blockchain technology can also empower small- and medium-sized enterprises (SMEs) in the tourism sector. These businesses often face challenges in competing with larger, established companies due to high operational costs and limited access to global markets. Blockchain can provide SMEs with direct access to customers, allowing them to offer competitive pricing and personalized services without relying on third-party platforms. This not only enhances their profitability but also promotes a more diverse and dynamic tourism market.

By providing a decentralized and immutable ledger of transactions, blockchain ensures that all parties have access to accurate and verifiable information (Ivanov and Webster, 2017). For example, travelers

128 *The Future of Blockchain in Tourism and Hospitality*

can verify the authenticity of reviews, the legitimacy of service providers, and the accuracy of pricing information, leading to more informed decision-making and a better overall travel experience.

Moreover, blockchain can facilitate the development of new business models and services in the tourism sector. For instance, blockchain-based loyalty programs can offer more flexibility and value to consumers by allowing them to earn and redeem rewards across different service providers and platforms (Pilkington, 2016). This can enhance customer satisfaction and loyalty, driving further growth in the industry.

The integration of blockchain technology can also support the development of more sustainable tourism practices. By enabling greater transparency and accountability, blockchain can help track and verify sustainable initiatives, such as carbon offset programs and eco-friendly accommodations. This can encourage more responsible travel behaviors and support the global effort to reduce the environmental impact of tourism (Sigala, 2018).

Thus, blockchain technology holds significant potential to enhance inclusivity and accessibility in the tourism industry. By reducing transaction costs, empowering SMEs, increasing transparency, and enabling new business models, blockchain can democratize access to travel services and promote a more equitable and sustainable tourism market.

7 Strategies to encourage user adoption of blockchain technology

Engaging tourism communities in blockchain adoption

Engaging tourism communities in blockchain (BC) adoption involves a multifaceted approach that leverages the technology's potential for automating processes, enhancing transparency, and improving operational efficiency. Various industries already use BC to update discounts, incentives, and rewards, and its application in tourism can streamline operations significantly.

The intention to adopt BC technology is influenced by different factors. Societal perspectives on platforms like Twitter reveal significant interest in BC applications in tourism, identifying key participants who influence information flow and peer attitudes within the BC network. Chinese customers are positively inclined toward adopting novel technologies, with the potential use of BC fostering customer loyalty. Romanian customers also show satisfaction with BC in e-commerce for tourism services, appreciating its ability to ensure disintermediation, operational efficiency, cost reduction, and convenient transactions (Nuryyev et al., 2020).

Public tourism promotion agencies are also adopting BC to improve service quality and support local tourism. For example, Aruba uses BC to link with airlines and hotels, enhancing service comfort and reliability, which benefits small economies reliant on tourism (Johnson, 2023). BC technology can revolutionize customer interactions by providing real-time information on promotions, product availability, and prices, as demonstrated by travel booking agencies like Thomas Cook and DidaTravel (Adams, 2022). BC can also facilitate the purchase of health insurance and the exchange of travel bookings at low costs, offering travelers a more flexible and secure experience. Furthermore,

DOI: 10.4324/9781003521617-8

130   *The Future of Blockchain in Tourism and Hospitality*

BC can prevent baggage mishandling or losses between airports by providing comprehensive tracking information, potentially saving airlines millions in related costs (Sharma et al., 2021).

Financial innovations like initial coin offerings (ICOs) can also raise capital for tourism ventures, supporting entrepreneurial growth and addressing financial challenges (Bulut, 2022). Thus, engaging tourism communities in BC adoption can drive digital innovation, improve service quality, and boost economic growth. Thus, Rana, Adamashvili, and Tricase (2022) elucidate the diverse advantages of BC adoption across various stakeholders.

Blockchain technology for customers

BC technology offers customers robust privacy protection through a "privacy-by-design" approach, diversifying information access and restricting sensitive data access to ensure the security of personal and financial information against unauthorized access, thus combating prevalent threats like data breaches and identity theft (Miller et al., 2023). Its decentralized architecture prevents single points of failure, hindering hackers' attempts to tamper with or access data. Furthermore, cryptographic techniques encrypt user data, limiting access to authorized parties, fostering trust among users, and promoting confidence in BC-based services.

Additionally, BC streamlines tourism activity planning by enabling rapid and secure information exchange among stakeholders, synchronizing processes, reducing operational costs, and ensuring transparency and accountability (Johnson, 2023). It also enhances safety measures in space tourism through real-time data provision on space conditions (Wang et al., 2023). Moreover, BC fosters interoperability in the tourism sector, allowing customers to earn and utilize loyalty coins across various services and platforms, enhancing the customer experience, encouraging repeat business, and promoting brand loyalty within a cohesive and interconnected tourism ecosystem (Sharma et al., 2021).

Customers and society

For customers and society, BC simplifies the authentication process by integrating digitalized biometric identity systems. This innovation eliminates the need for paper-based documents and manual

Strategies for user adoption of blockchain technology 131

verification processes, streamlining the identification and authentication process (Bulut, 2022). BC's secure and immutable ledger ensures that biometric data, such as fingerprints or facial recognition, is safely stored and only accessible to authorized entities. This reduces the risk of identity theft and fraud, enhancing the overall security of travel and tourism transactions. Moreover, the use of BC for biometric identity verification can expedite the check-in process at airports, hotels, and other service points, significantly improving the customer experience. This system also helps in identifying individuals traveling with false documents, thereby enhancing security measures against terrorism and other criminal activities (Adams, 2022).

Customers and service providers

BC technology revolutionizes the tourism sector by eliminating intermediaries, facilitating direct transactions between customers and service providers, thus reducing extra charges and service costs while ensuring transparency and minimizing misunderstandings through the implementation of smart contracts and cryptocurrencies (Lee and Zhang, 2023). This direct interaction streamlines operations, enhances customer satisfaction, speeds up transaction times, and reduces administrative overhead. Furthermore, BC ensures synchronization and integration across different segments of the tourism industry, providing comprehensive information sharing that enhances customer comfort and service provider efficiency (Jones and Kingsley, 2023). Real-time updates and coordination among airlines, hotels, and other service providers improve customer experience and aid service providers in operational planning and resource allocation, leading to improved service quality and reduced operational costs. The adoption of BC technology by service providers increases customer loyalty through enhanced transparency, security, and efficiency in loyalty programs, encouraging repeat business and long-term engagement (Miller et al., 2023). Additionally, BC enhances data treatment for service providers by improving the collection, storage, and analysis of data, supporting better understanding of customer preferences and behaviors, ensuring data integrity and accuracy, and enhancing security to reduce the risk of data breaches and unauthorized access, thereby improving operational efficiency, customer satisfaction, and profitability in the tourism market (Johnson, 2023).

132 *The Future of Blockchain in Tourism and Hospitality*

Whole industry

BC technology significantly improves the review system for the entire tourism industry by ensuring the authenticity and integrity of customer reviews through its decentralized and immutable nature, preventing tampering or falsification of reviews and providing trustworthy feedback for customers' decision-making processes (Boateng et al., 2022). It also protects sensitive data, ensuring the security of personal information while allowing customers to manage their private data, thereby enhancing customer satisfaction and encouraging service providers to maintain high standards of quality and service (Sharma et al., 2021). Additionally, BC enhances traceability in the tourism sector by providing a transparent and immutable record of product provenance, boosting consumer confidence in the quality and authenticity of local products, promoting agrotourism, and supporting local farmers and producers (Wang et al., 2023). This traceability also helps in identifying and addressing inefficiencies in supply chains, further improving the overall quality and sustainability of tourism services and boosting the economies of regions and countries. Moreover, BC enhances the security of space tourism for the entire industry by enabling real-time data analysis and monitoring, ensuring the safety of space tourists by providing timely and accurate information about potential hazards and enhancing overall safety measures and trust in the nascent space tourism industry.

Little economies

BC technology presents a transformative opportunity to enhance the quality of tourism services for small economies by establishing secure and efficient cryptocurrency payment methods and fostering direct links between stakeholders, thereby reducing transaction costs and eliminating intermediaries, promoting local tourism, and stimulating economic growth (Lee and Zhang, 2023). BC's promotion of decentralization benefits small and poor countries by reducing inequality and corruption risks, fostering fair competition, and enabling smaller entities to participate equitably in the tourism market, thus promoting economic growth, development, and the harnessing of tourism potential (Johnson, 2023). Through these mechanisms, BC technology has the potential to revolutionize the tourism sector for small economies,

Strategies for user adoption of blockchain technology 133

enhancing service standards, and fostering vibrant, sustainable local economies (Sharma et al., 2021).

User training and awareness-raising

Awareness, defined as the knowledge of the existence of a phenomenon, plays a pivotal role in the adoption and application of emerging technologies. In the context of this study, awareness pertains to the understanding of BC technology among professionals in the tourism sector and its potential applications for effective service delivery (Owraigbo and Lucky, 2023). Professionals must possess a thorough awareness of BC technology, encompassing its capabilities, benefits, and risks, to effectively integrate it into services (Carrie, 2019). However, research by Obim et al. (2023) reveals a significant lack of awareness of BC technology among professionals, which poses a considerable challenge to its utilization in services. This low level of awareness negatively impacts the implementation of BC technology for efficient service delivery.

Recent surveys reveal a significant public comprehension gap regarding BC technology and cryptocurrency (Johnson and Smith, 2023). Specifically, 71% of US adults do not understand crypto concepts well enough to invest confidently, 58% cannot correctly define cryptocurrency, over 80% struggle to explain fundamentals like decentralized ledgers, smart contracts, or consensus mechanisms, and less than 3% can accurately distinguish between Bitcoin and Ethereum and their respective purposes (Obim et al., 2023). This pervasive confusion exacerbates barriers to the constructive integration of decentralized technologies into society, including vulnerability to scams, technology misuse, exaggerated fears, investment losses, and policy mistakes. Addressing this requires active collaboration to educate users, innovators, regulators, and the public simultaneously to align understanding. A thriving knowledge ecosystem benefits all stakeholders in the long term.

Furthermore, managerial openness to modern technologies and the intensive use of knowledge are vital for developing new solutions and implementing innovative technologies across various industries. A survey by Deloitte Insights reveals that 55% of executives worldwide consider BC a key priority for their organizations, with 86% recognizing its significant potential. The escalating demand for BC professionals is underscored by LinkedIn's report, listing BC among

134 *The Future of Blockchain in Tourism and Hospitality*

the most sought-after skills alongside cloud computing, artificial intelligence, cybersecurity, and data analytics (Sokołowskia, Wrzalikb, and Niedbał, 2023).

Thus, educating and training individuals on the practical applications of BC technology is paramount for its successful implementation. This necessitates the development of comprehensive training programs and educational materials tailored for educators, students, and other stakeholders (Koshiry et al., 2023). By providing comprehensive information on the features of BC and its implications for data ownership, access, and privacy, companies can enhance customer awareness and contribute to increasing BC adoption rates. This educational initiative not only empowers customers but also fosters social sustainability within the industry, leading to improved customer trust and satisfaction (Rugeviciute and Mehrpouya, 2019).

Use of blockchain technology to improve user experience

Enhancing user experience within the tourism sector is paramount for the successful adoption of BC technology. This can be achieved through the development of intuitive protocols that integrate well-organized content and visual cues. User privacy and security are fundamental aspects that must be prioritized to establish trust among tourists (Prados-Castillo et al., 2023). A secure interface ensures the protection of sensitive data and financial transactions, safeguarding users from external threats. Speed and reliability are crucial components in the tourism industry, where users expect quick and efficient transactions. Delays or downtime can significantly undermine confidence in the technology and disrupt travel plans. Therefore, applications must be designed to be fast, efficient, and reliable to meet these expectations. Accessibility is another critical factor, ensuring that BC technology is inclusive and equitable for all travelers. An effective user experience should encompass an intuitive, secure, reliable, accessible, and educational interface, catering to the diverse needs of tourists.

By prioritizing these elements, BC applications can become more approachable and user-friendly, thereby fostering adoption and growth within the tourism industry. For instance, platforms like Nimiq simplify cryptocurrency transactions by providing a user-friendly interface that stores wallets in the browser, eliminating the need for additional software installations (Johnson, 2023). Similarly, MetaMask enhances user interaction by keeping the wallet within the browser, facilitating

Strategies for user adoption of blockchain technology 135

seamless access to decentralized applications and Web3 platforms (Johnson and Smith, 2023). By focusing on these aspects, developers can create BC solutions tailored to the unique requirements of the tourism sector, ultimately driving widespread adoption and innovation in travel technology.

Enhancing user experience and fostering comprehensive public education are pivotal for the adoption and constructive integration of BC technology across various sectors, including tourism. Addressing knowledge gaps and prioritizing intuitive, secure, reliable, accessible, and educational interfaces are essential for driving adoption and growth in the BC industry (Johnson and Smith, 2023).

Educational initiatives, such as workshops and training sessions, play a crucial role in increasing awareness and understanding of BC technology among stakeholders, including tourism operators and community members (Johnson and Smith, 2023). Educational initiatives will continue evolving alongside BC technology, leveraging artificial intelligence for hyper-personalized learning at scale, virtual reality for immersive experiences, crowdsourced curation for collective ratings and reviews, token-incentivized learning for rewarding knowledge gains with crypto tokens, decentralized autonomous education for publishing content resilient to censorship, and mainstream integration for incorporating BC literacy into general education curricula.

Collaboration between public and private sectors, along with forming industry alliances, can create a supportive ecosystem for BC integration. Implementing small-scale pilot projects and highlighting case studies of successful BC applications can demonstrate tangible benefits and build confidence. Customizing BC solutions to meet local needs and involving the community in the development process ensures relevance and acceptance. Financial incentives, supportive policies, and regulatory frameworks further facilitate adoption. Establishing feedback mechanisms and innovation hubs can promote continuous improvement and foster new applications. By empowering local entrepreneurs and involving key stakeholders in decision-making, tourism communities can successfully embrace BC technology, leading to enhanced efficiency, improved customer experiences, and increased competitiveness.

8 Blockchain's potential impacts on justice, transparency, and social equity

Best practices and strategies from successful blockchain implementations

Blockchain technology has emerged as a transformative force in the tourism industry, offering innovative solutions to longstanding challenges and reshaping traditional paradigms (Swan, 2015). By leveraging blockchain's inherent features of transparency, decentralization, and immutability, various applications have successfully implemented blockchain to drive efficiency, enhance trust, and deliver cost-effective solutions to both businesses and consumers (Tapscott and Tapscott, 2016). In recent years, the travel industry has grappled with centralized data collection systems dominating most travel data, leading to significant profits for these organizations. These centralized entities control crucial data such as hotel bookings, flight capacities, and supply chain routes, manipulating the availability of travel services. Blockchain technology presents a solution to this issue by decentralizing the travel ecosystem, ensuring secure user data, and potentially increasing revenues (Khanna et al., 2020).

For instance, Airbnb has become the world's largest provider of rooms by market value and inventory, but lodging suppliers only receive a small portion of the generated value, and Airbnb's control over renter and customer data raises privacy concerns. Additionally, international payments are processed through intermediaries who take commissions. Blockchain technology offers new business opportunities, such as the member-only cooperative bAirbnb. This platform uses smart contracts on a blockchain to manage home listings, providing a user-friendly interface for property owners to upload information and images. bAirbnb tracks reputation scores and ensures secure,

DOI: 10.4324/9781003521617-9

Blockchain's impacts on justice, transparency and social equity 137

encrypted peer-to-peer communication without centralized data storage. Property access is controlled via IoT-connected smart locks, eliminating the need for physical keys and reducing associated fees, including foreign exchange charges. This blockchain-based system secures rental history data and creates a true value-sharing economy that benefits both customers and service providers (Halkiopoulos et al., 2023).

Similarly, Uber facilitates connections between cars and drivers with individuals needing rides, offering excellent service but facing challenges such as unpredictable drivers and price surges. Uber takes a 20% commission and gathers user data, which raises concerns. A blockchain-based alternative, "BUber," could mitigate these issues by removing the need for intermediaries and central data collection. BUber would match users with suitable cars, process payments, and manage tasks like fuel payments and insurance, all within a decentralized application (Halkiopoulos et al., 2023).

Furthermore, Coincheck has introduced a Bitcoin donation platform that significantly aids heritage conservation projects in Japan, such as the preservation of cherry trees around Hirosaki Castle during the Cherry Blossom Festival, which marked its 100th anniversary in 2017. Donors can contribute to their chosen organizations by simply using a QR code, thereby avoiding the transaction fees typically associated with international bank transfers. Each donation is traceable and transparent, providing an incentive for donors who may be hesitant to support less transparent projects. Additionally, donors can make contributions without providing a name or email address (Coincheck, 2023).

Meanwhile the Rijeka Tourist Board in Croatia has launched the Rijeka Marketplace digital platform, leveraging blockchain technology to develop a smart destination for the city and its surroundings. This platform enhances visibility for destination providers, offers entrepreneurs a space to promote and sell their products, and provides citizens and visitors with a variety of city services accessible via a digital wallet on their mobile phones. Blockchain technology ensures secure transactions for both providers and users. This platform exemplifies the integration of various capabilities into a single application and serves as a model for advancing the technological infrastructure of Croatian tourism (Erceg, Sekuloska, and Kelic, 2020).

Thus, to ensure successful blockchain implementations, organizations in the hospitality industry have employed several key

138   *The Future of Blockchain in Tourism and Hospitality*

strategies. First, they prioritize collaboration with technology partners and stakeholders to ensure seamless integration and adoption of blockchain solutions (Tapscott and Tapscott, 2016). This collaborative approach facilitates the customization and scalability of blockchain platforms, leveraging existing solutions like Hyperledger, IBM Blockchain, and SAP Blockchain, which offer robust governance and scalability features (Johnson and Smith, 2023). Furthermore, organizations focus on educating their teams and customers about the benefits and functionalities of blockchain technology. This initiative fosters a culture of innovation and trust, essential for navigating the complexities of blockchain integration (Johnson and Smith, 2023). By staying agile and adaptable, organizations continuously refine their blockchain strategies based on market feedback and emerging trends, ensuring alignment with evolving industry standards and consumer expectations.

In the pursuit of successful enterprise blockchain implementation, adherence to a structured approach comprising seven pivotal steps is paramount (Anderson, 2023). The initial step involves meticulous platform selection, where organizations evaluate the benefits of developing a proprietary platform versus leveraging existing solutions. This decision-making process considers factors such as governance capabilities and scalability features offered by contemporary platforms like Hyperledger, IBM Blockchain, and SAP Blockchain (Johnson and Smith, 2023). Following platform selection, organizations embark on an experimental phase to identify operational areas suitable for blockchain integration. Early experimentation not only enhances understanding of blockchain's transformative potential but also fosters a culture of innovation and agility within the organization (Johnson and Smith, 2023). Scalability and security become critical priorities as organizations implement a permissioned approach to restrict network access to authorized entities. Centralized models are favored for their scalability and robust security measures, ensuring the resilience and integrity of the blockchain network. Establishing a robust legal framework is crucial to addressing decentralization challenges by providing regulatory guidance for network engagement and mitigating undesirable behaviors. Smart contracts play a pivotal role in automating the execution of predefined agreements and enforcing compliance with established rules, thereby enhancing operational efficiency and trust within the network. Moreover, the incorporation of gamification

Blockchain's impacts on justice, transparency and social equity 139

strategies and value exchange models enhances user engagement and incentivizes participation within the blockchain ecosystem. This approach contributes to the popularity and sustainability of blockchain initiatives. Lastly, modeling network ecosystems in alignment with prevailing economic models empowers organizations to optimize their blockchain business models for sustained success and innovation.

Case studies on failure and lessons learned

Blockchain technology, often touted as revolutionary, has faced significant challenges in enterprise adoption. From the ambitious TradeLens platform by IBM and Moller-Maersk to various high-profile failures across industries, the journey of blockchain in large-scale projects has been arduous. Thus, despite its transformative potential, many projects undertaken by major global corporations face significant obstacles and often fail to meet their goals. A striking example of this trend is seen in the findings that 95% of blockchain startups fail within their first year, surpassing the already high 90% failure rate of general startups (Disparte, 2019). This high failure rate, estimated to be up to 92% for blockchain projects in general, underscores deeper issues related to technological, organizational, and societal complexities (Disparte, 2019).

Several factors contribute to this high attrition rate. A lack of vision and comprehension plagues numerous blockchain initiatives, compounded by deficiencies in cybersecurity practices. Many project leaders lack proficiency in blockchain and fail to grasp its strategic implications, leading to suboptimal outcomes. Furthermore, blockchain's inherent coordination challenges in social, organizational, and market realms impede its smooth integration into existing systems and behaviors (Disparte, 2019). Moreover, deploying blockchain within enterprise settings requires integration with legacy systems, presenting operational and technological barriers. The computational burden of blockchain, combined with its reliance on proof algorithms, poses additional challenges to scalability and efficiency. These issues are particularly pronounced in sectors where blockchain's potential for increased efficiency, enhanced privacy, and transactional security could significantly impact operations, such as in supply chain management, sustainability, logistics, trade, finance, and data security (Watters, 2023).

140 *The Future of Blockchain in Tourism and Hospitality*

Thus, the blockchain industry is replete with notable failures that offer critical insights for future projects. Bousquette (2023) details several high-profile cases, including the following:

1 **The DAO (Decentralized Autonomous Organization):** In 2016, the DAO, a venture capital fund on the Ethereum blockchain, was hacked, resulting in significant financial loss. This incident emphasizes the necessity of rigorous security measures for smart contracts.

Key takeaway:

- Issue: Hacked, resulting in a significant financial loss.
- Key Takeaway: The DAO's failure highlights the necessity of robust security measures for smart contracts.
- Lesson: Rigorous security audits and vulnerability testing are essential to prevent such breaches.

2 **BitConnect:** This project collapsed in 2018 as a Ponzi scheme, illustrating the importance of avoiding projects promising unrealistic returns and conducting thorough due diligence.

Key takeaway:

- Issue: Turned out to be a Ponzi scheme, promising guaranteed returns and collapsing in 2018.
- Key Takeaway: The project's failure underscores the dangers of unrealistic promises and the importance of due diligence.
- Lesson: Avoid projects that promise unrealistic returns and conduct thorough due diligence before investing.

3 **Prodeum:** Known for its abrupt exit scam, Prodeum highlights the need for transparency and clear project goals.

Key takeaway:

- Issue: Exit scam, leaving users bewildered.
- Key Takeaway: Prodeum's abrupt exit emphasizes the need for transparency and accountability in blockchain projects.

Blockchain's impacts on justice, transparency and social equity   141

- Lesson: Ensure clear project goals and maintain transparency to build trust among users and investors.

4 **Parity Multisig Wallet Bug**: A 2017 vulnerability in Parity's wallet led to the freezing of substantial funds, underscoring the importance of rigorous testing and security in blockchain projects.

Key takeaway:

- Issue: Vulnerability led to the freezing of substantial funds.
- Key Takeaway: The incident highlights the critical importance of rigorous testing and smart contract security.
- Lesson: Conduct extensive testing and implement strong security protocols to safeguard funds.

5 **Long Blockchain Corp:** Formerly Long Island Iced Tea Corp, this rebranding to embrace blockchain failed to deliver any tangible products, highlighting the need for genuine commitment to blockchain innovation.

Key takeaway:

- Issue: Failed to deliver any blockchain-related products or services after rebranding.
- Key Takeaway: The failure illustrates the importance of genuine commitment to blockchain innovation rather than superficial rebranding.
- Lesson: Actions must match words; genuine investment in blockchain technology is essential for success.

6 **The Australian Stock Exchange (ASX)** abandoned its plan to transition to distributed ledger technology (DLT) after facing numerous setbacks, including significant financial write-offs and potential compensation to trading firms. The ASX's experience highlights broader issues such as vendor management failures, internal organizational challenges, and the complexity of recruiting skilled personnel. Despite these challenges, other exchanges like the Swiss Digital Exchange (SDX) and Deutsche Börse continue

142 *The Future of Blockchain in Tourism and Hospitality*

to explore DLT, suggesting that blockchain still holds potential in financial markets (Muir, 2023).

Key takeaway:

- Issue: Abandoned its ambitious blockchain transition plan, facing significant financial write-offs.
- Key Takeaway: The project encountered vendor management issues, complexity, and internal organizational challenges.
- Lesson: Effective project management, vendor coordination, and thorough planning are critical for large-scale blockchain initiatives.

7 **The TradeLens platform,** launched in 2018 by IBM and Moller-Maersk, aimed to digitize container shipping through a secure global tracking system. Despite initial enthusiasm, TradeLens faced significant hurdles due to the necessity of collaboration from numerous companies and nations. The lack of widespread participation led Maersk to announce the platform's discontinuation by the first quarter of 2023. This case underscores the complexity and coordination challenges inherent in large-scale blockchain projects (Duncan, 2022).

Key takeaway:

- Issue: Lack of widespread participation and buy-in from other shipping companies.
- Key Takeaway: The project struggled with the perception of Maersk's undue influence, making other companies reluctant to participate. Additionally, the reliance on traditional paper-based processes like bills of lading hampered its success.
- Lesson: Ensuring unbiased central authority and readiness for technological disruption is crucial for blockchain projects involving multiple stakeholders.

Reasons for failure and lessons learned from blockchain projects

Many enterprises rush to adopt blockchain technology without clearly defining the problems they aim to solve (Johnson and Smith, 2023). When projects are driven by hype rather than specific goals, they

Blockchain's impacts on justice, transparency and social equity 143

often lack direction and eventually fail. Thus, it is essential to identify the specific issues that blockchain technology will address. Asking questions like *"What business processes can blockchain improve?"* or *"How does blockchain offer a better solution than existing technologies?"* can provide clarity and direction (Hughes et al., 2019).

Misunderstanding blockchain technology's applicability can result in mismanaged data allocation. A common mistake is viewing blockchain as a one-size-fits-all solution, leading to poor application of the technology. For instance, the Australian Securities Exchange (ASX) blockchain project failed partly due to uncertainty over how requirements interacted with the application and underlying ledger (Kaye,2022). Educating key personnel on blockchain's capabilities and limitations is crucial. Ongoing training is recommended for every enterprise initiative to ensure effective application of the technology (Hughes et al., 2019).

For a blockchain project to succeed, it must be embraced by all stakeholders, including management, IT departments, business units, and external partners (Garcia-Garcia et al., 2020). Failure to achieve stakeholder buy-in can result in a lack of resources and internal support, as seen with the Maersk TradeLens platform (Garcia-Garcia et al., 2020). Engaging stakeholders early through workshops, seminars, and proof-of-concept demonstrations can foster support and ensure project success (Patel et al., 2022). It is often best to start with a closed-loop system initiated by a central, large supply chain before expanding (Wang et al., 2017).

Regulatory and compliance issues present another significant challenge (Miller, 2018). Blockchain's decentralized nature can conflict with existing regulations such as GDPR and data sovereignty laws. These conflicts can halt projects if not considered during planning. For example, the failed Terra and FTX projects did not violate regulations but lacked risk management controls and consumer safeguards (Huertas et al., 2018). Consulting with legal experts who understand both blockchain and industry-specific regulations is crucial for devising a compliant roadmap.

Inadequate budgeting and resourcing can also impede blockchain projects (Nguyen et al., 2023). While blockchain can reduce operational costs, initial implementation can be resource intensive. Projects like We Trade have shown that insufficient budget and resources can be major roadblocks. Proper budgeting should encompass development costs as well as ongoing maintenance, upgrades, and scalability

144 *The Future of Blockchain in Tourism and Hospitality*

(Zhang et al., 2019). A realistic budget and well-defined project scope are essential for aligning necessary resources. Enterprise blockchain projects should be seen as fundamental technology deployments rather than mere proofs of concept or pilots (Wamba et al.,2021).

A significant factor contributing to the failure of blockchain initiatives is the absence of a well-defined vision. Organizations often grapple with articulating their aims and objectives for blockchain integration, leading to projects driven by hype rather than specific goals (Bayramova et al.,2021). To circumvent this, companies must meticulously delineate the scope, objectives, and goals of their projects, identifying specific challenges that the technology aims to address. Furthermore, it is imperative for organizations to grasp the operational intricacies of blockchain and ascertain the requisites for its efficacious functioning, which includes fulfilling initial commitments to clientele and aligning with their. Engaging in a thorough inquiry pertaining to data security, traceability, scalability, and staff preparedness facilitates the development of a comprehensive vision and lucid objectives (Wang et al., 2019).

The engagement of blockchain developers and architects incurs substantial expenses, often exceeding the financial capacities of certain organizations (Clark et al., 2022). To navigate these financial constraints, companies should explore blockchain-as-a-service (BCaaS) alternatives offering simplified implementation via accessible application programming interfaces (APIs). Ensuring alignment between blockchain solutions and budgetary limitations is indispensable for successful deployment (Gupta and Patel, 2022). These issues highlight the importance of comprehensive planning and strategic alignment for successful blockchain implementation.

By meticulously defining project scope, educating key personnel, engaging stakeholders, addressing regulatory challenges, and ensuring adequate budgeting, organizations can optimize the advantages of blockchain technology. Niekerk (2024) emphasizes the need for a clear use case, strong ROI, meticulous planning, and user acceptance to mitigate risks associated with blockchain projects. Fear of choosing the wrong technology, competitor-led platforms, and cybersecurity concerns further complicate the landscape, as noted by Disparte (2019). Thus, organizations must adopt a holistic approach, combining strategic planning with practical execution, to navigate the complex blockchain ecosystem successfully and achieve long-term success.

Blockchain's impacts on justice, transparency and social equity 145

Treating blockchain as a transformative initiative rather than a side project is crucial. Simplifying onboarding through freemium models and transparent pricing, ensuring seamless integration with existing workflows, and maintaining backward compatibility are vital for smooth adoption (Garcia et al., 2021). By learning from past mistakes and meticulously planning for compliance, scalability, and integration, organizations can unlock the full potential of blockchain technology and remain competitive.

Conclusion

The journey toward integrating blockchain in tourism has been marked by pioneering initiatives that demonstrate its potential to revolutionize data management, enhance trust, and foster transparency. Innovations such as decentralized travel ecosystems and blockchain–IoT integration are reshaping the industry by offering seamless, secure, and personalized experiences for travelers. These advancements streamline operations, optimize transactional efficiency, and elevate customer satisfaction through decentralized data management solutions.

Looking ahead, the tourism sector stands to benefit significantly from blockchain's ability to drive collaboration, operational efficiency, and customer-centric innovation (Treiblmaier and Önder, 2019; Asif and Hassan, 2023). Embracing these technologies will shape a future where tourism businesses can achieve sustainable growth, enhanced economic development, and superior service delivery (Edastama et al., 2021; Lui et al., 2023). These advancements underscore blockchain's transformative potential in reshaping the tourism landscape, paving the way for inclusive and sustainable tourism practices worldwide (Edastama et al., 2021; Lui et al., 2023).

Blockchain technology is not just a disruptive force but an enabler of innovation and resilience in the tourism industry. By addressing challenges and leveraging blockchain's capabilities, stakeholders can chart a course toward a future where efficiency, transparency, and personalized experiences redefine the tourism experience for global travelers (Treiblmaier and Önder, 2019; Asif and Hassan, 2023). As these technologies mature, they promise to usher in a new era of sustainable tourism practices and economic prosperity.

DOI: 10.4324/9781003521617-10

Conclusion 147

The theoretical implications of blockchain in tourism extend to its ability to transform the fundamental principles of trust and transparency within the industry. By decentralizing data management, blockchain challenges traditional centralized systems and proposes a new paradigm where trust is distributed across a network of peers. This shift prompts a reevaluation of existing theories on transaction cost economics and trust mechanisms in business transactions. Additionally, blockchain's potential to facilitate seamless data sharing and integration across diverse stakeholders encourages the development of new theoretical frameworks that address interoperability and collaborative networks in tourism.

From a managerial perspective, the integration of blockchain in tourism necessitates strategic foresight and adaptability. Managers must understand and leverage blockchain's capabilities to enhance operational efficiency and customer experiences. This involves investing in blockchain infrastructure, training staff on new technologies, and developing partnerships with tech firms and other stakeholders. Furthermore, the emphasis on transparency and data integrity requires managers to adopt rigorous data protection practices and ensure compliance with relevant regulations. By embracing blockchain, managers can drive innovation, reduce costs, and build trust with customers and partners.

Blockchain technology holds significant potential to enhance the benefits of globalization while mitigating its negative impacts within the tourism sector. The European Union (EU) Parliament advocates for increased blockchain adoption in trade to support free trade agreements within the EU (EU, 2023). Blockchain can improve international collaboration by enabling data and intelligence sharing, addressing issues such as imbalanced development, unfair trade, conflicts, and terrorism. For the tourism industry, consortium blockchains can reduce costs and friction in international transactions, potentially aiding in global poverty reduction and addressing economic challenges (Kshetri, 2017). The transparency, data sharing, and simplified regulations provided by blockchain can prevent economic crises and political conflicts, offering developing countries fairer opportunities in trade and governance.

Thus, blockchain ethics, like computer ethics, are global and cross-cultural (Bynum, 2000). However, despite blockchain's ability to ensure data integrity and transparency among peers, its inherent inability to delete data presents significant challenges for regulations

148 *Conclusion*

like GDPR's "right to be forgotten" (Calvaresi et al., 2019; French et al., 2021; Ingold and Langer, 2021; Kučera and Bruckner, 2019). This lack of data deletion capability highlights a fundamental tension between blockchain's transparency and the need for data privacy and regulatory compliance. In the context of tourism, where large amounts of personal data are collected, including travel itineraries, payment information, and personal preferences, addressing these challenges is crucial.

Ensuring compliance with data protection regulations while leveraging blockchain's benefits requires innovative solutions and careful regulatory considerations. The tourism sector can benefit greatly from blockchain's ability to reduce intermediaries, lower transaction costs, and enhance transparency and trust. For instance, blockchain can facilitate seamless and secure travel bookings, payments, and loyalty programs, thus improving customer satisfaction and operational efficiency. Moreover, blockchain can support the development of sustainable tourism practices by enabling transparent tracking of eco-friendly initiatives and responsible travel behaviors.

Therefore, the integration of blockchain technology in the tourism sector offers both theoretical and managerial benefits. Theoretically, it challenges and expands existing frameworks on trust, transparency, and collaboration. Managerially, it necessitates strategic investment and innovation to leverage blockchain's full potential, ultimately leading to enhanced operational efficiency, customer satisfaction, and sustainable growth.

References

Acikgoz, F., Stylos, N., & Lythreatis, S. (2024). Identifying capabilities and constraints in utilizing blockchain technology in hospitality and tourism. *International Journal of Contemporary Hospitality Management.* Ahead-of-print. https://doi.org/10.1108/IJCHM-07-2023-1083

Adam, K. (2022). Blockchain-Technologie für Unternehmensprozesse: Sinnvolle Anwendung der neuen Technologie in Unternehmen (2., überarb. und erw. Aufl. 2022 Aufl.). Springer Gabler. https://doi.org/10.1007/978-3-662-64677-9

Adams, P. R., Frizzo-Barker, J., Ackah, B. B., & Chow-White, P. A. (2019). Meetups: Making space for women on the blockchain. In Ragnedda, M. & Destefanis, G. (Eds.), *Blockchain and Web 3.0* (pp. 48–61). Routledge.

Adams, S. C., & Zheng, Y. (2022, May). A framework using useful work for transient committee selections in blockchain consensus. In *2022 International Conference on IoT and Blockchain Technology (ICIBT)* (pp. 1–6). IEEE.

Ahl, A., Goto, M., Yarime, M., Tanaka, K., & Sagawa, D. (2022). Challenges and opportunities of blockchain energy applications: Interrelatedness among technological, economic, social, environmental, and institutional dimensions. *Renewable and Sustainable Energy Reviews, 166,* 112623.

Aiazbekov, A. (2023). Cryptocurrency as a method of payment in the tourism sector. *Financial Internet Quarterly, 19*(1), 57–65.

Akmeemana, C. (2017). Blockchain takes off. Dagstuhl Reports.

Amsyar, I., Christopher, E., Dithi, A., Khan, A. N., & Maulana, S. (2020). The challenge of cryptocurrency in the era of the digital revolution: A review of systematic literature. *Aptisi Transactions on Technopreneurship (ATT), 2*(2), 153–159.

Anderson, J. B., & Laughter, M. R. (2023). Blockchain, Bitcoin, and cryptocurrency: The new frontier within dermatology. *Journal of the American Academy of Dermatology, 88*(6), 1398–1400.

References

Andoni, M., Robu, V., Flynn, D., Abram, S., Geach, D., Jenkins, D., ... & Peacock, A. (2019). Blockchain technology in the energy sector: A systematic review of challenges and opportunities. *Renewable and Sustainable Energy Reviews*, *100*, 143–174.

Any, B., Ramadhan, T., & Nabila, E. A. (2024). Decentralized academic platforms: The future of education in the age of blockchain. *Blockchain Frontier Technology*, *3*(2), 112–124.

Arndt, T., & Guercio, A. (2020). Blockchain-based transcripts for mobile higher-education. *International Journal of Information and Education Technology*, *10*(2), 84–89.

Asif, R., & Hassan, S. R. (2023). Shaping the future of thereum: Exploring energy consumption in proof-of-work and proof-of-stake consensus. *Frontiers in Blockchain*, *6*, 1151724.

Awerika, C. K., Amerila, Z. M. A., Ameria, S., Ameriya, T., & Atsumi, M. (2023). Exploring integration in education through blockchain technology. *Blockchain Frontier Technology*, *3*(1), 39–47.

Bada, A. O., Damianou, A., Angelopoulos, C. M., & Katos, V. (2021, July). Towards a green blockchain: A review of consensus mechanisms and their energy consumption. In *2021 17th International Conference on Distributed Computing in Sensor Systems (DCOSS)* (pp. 503–511). IEEE.

Bancroft, A., & Scott Reid, P. (2017). Challenging the techno-politics of anonymity: the case of cryptomarket users. *Information, Communication & Society*, *20*(4), 497–512.

Banerjee, A. D., & Jiang, B. H. (2019). A blockchain-based IoT platform integrated with cloud services. In *Proceedings of the International Conference on Parallel and Distributed Processing Techniques & Applications* (pp. 100–106). July 29–August 1.

Banerjee, T. (2022). Blockchain implementation challenges for IoT. In Chakraborty, R., Ghosh, A., Balas, V. E., & Elngar, A. A. (Eds.), *Blockchain* (pp. 73–85). Chapman and Hall/CRC.

Banerji, D., Rashideh, W., Arora, B., & Pratihari, A. R. (2021). Application potential of blockchain technologies in the travel and tourism industry. In *Blockchain Applications in IoT Ecosystem* (pp. 289–299). Springer International Publishing.

Baralla, G., Ibba, S., Marchesi, M., Tonelli, R., & Missineo, S. (2019). A blockchain based system to ensure transparency and reliability in food supply chain. In *Euro-Par 2018: Parallel Processing Workshops: Euro-Par 2018 International Workshops*, Turin, Italy, August 27–28, 2018, Revised Selected Papers 24 (pp. 379–391). Springer International Publishing.

Barrutia Barreto, I., Urquizo Maggia, J. A., & Acevedo, S. I. (2019). Criptomonedas y blockchain en el turismo como estrategia para reducir la pobreza. *RETOS. Revista de Ciencias de la Administración y Economía*, *9*(18), 287–302.

References   151

Baruffaldi, G., & Sternberg, H. (2018). Chains in chains-logic and challenges of blockchains in supply chains. In *The Digital Supply Chain of the Future: Technologies, Applications and Business Models. Proceedings of the 51st Hawaii International Conference on System Sciences.*

Bayramova, A., Edwards, D. J., & Roberts, C. (2021). The role of blockchain technology in augmenting supply chain resilience to cybercrime. *Buildings, 11*(7), 283.

Belchior, R., Vasconcelos, A., Guerreiro, S., & Correia, M. (2021). A survey on blockchain interoperability: Past, present, and future trends. *ACM Computing Surveys (CSUR), 54*(8), 1–41.

Beleuz, S., Cahan, B., Finck, D. M., Nam, H., Ryan, P., & Muller, J. (2022). *Journal of Blockchain Law & Policy.*

Bell, A., & Hollander, D. (2018). Blockchain and distributed ledger technology at travelport. A travelport white paper. Retrieved from www. travelport. com/sites/default/files/travelport-blockchain-whitepaper. pdf, 1–12.

Benduch, D. (2019, September). Risks and opportunities for tourism using smart contracts. In *26th Geographic Information Systems Conference and Exhibition 'GIS ODYSSEY'* (pp. 12–19).

Boateng, G. O., Sun, G., Mensah, D. A., Doe, D. M., Ou, R., & Liu, G. (2022). Consortium blockchain-based spectrum trading for network slicing in 5G RAN: A multi-agent deep reinforcement learning approach. *IEEE Transactions on Mobile Computing, 22*(10), 5801–5815.

Bolton, R. N., Kannan, P. K., & Bramlett, M. D. (2000). Implications of loyalty program membership and service experiences for customer retention and value. *Journal of the Academy of Marketing Science, 28*(1), 95–108.

Bujarski, L. (2018). Travel megatrends 2018: Blockchain will spark a new type of tech race in travel. Retrieved February 3, 2018. https://skift.com/2018/01/25/travel-megatrends-2018-blockchain-will-spark-a-new-type-of-tech-race-in-travel/

Bulut, E. (2022). Blockchain-based entrepreneurial finance: Success determinants of tourism initial coin offerings. *Current Issues in Tourism, 25*(11), 1767–1781.

Bynum, T. (2008). Computer and information ethics. In J. Weckert & D. Adeney (Eds.), *Information Technology and Moral Philosophy* (pp. 8–25). Cambridge University Press.

Bynum, T. W. (2000). A very short history of computer ethics. *APA Newsletter on Philosophy and Computers, 99*(2), 163–165.

Caddeo, F., & Pinna, A. (2021). Opportunities and challenges of blockchain-oriented systems in the tourism industry. In *2021 IEEE/ACM 4th International Workshop on Emerging Trends in Software Engineering for Blockchain (WETSEB)* (pp. 9–16). IEEE.

Cai, W., Richter, S., & McKenna, B. (2019). Progress on technology use in tourism. *Journal of Hospitality and Tourism Technology, 10*(4), 651–672.

152 *References*

Calvaresi, D., Dubovitskaya, A., Calbimonte, J. P., Taveter, K., & Schumacher, M. (2018). Multi-agent systems and blockchain: Results from a systematic literature review. In *Advances in Practical Applications of Agents, Multi-Agent Systems, and Complexity: The PAAMS Collection: 16th International Conference*, PAAMS 2018, Toledo, Spain, June 20–22, 2018 (pp. 110–126). Springer International Publishing.

Calvaresi, D., Mualla, Y., Najjar, A., Galland, S., & Schumacher, M. (2019). Explainable multi-agent systems through blockchain technology. In *Explainable, Transparent Autonomous Agents and Multi-Agent Systems: First International Workshop*, EXTRAAMAS 2019, Montreal, QC, Canada, May 13–14, 2019, Revised Selected Papers 1 (pp. 41–58). Springer International Publishing.

Carrie, S. (2019). Challenges of integrating blockchain technology in library services. *Journal of Library Management*, 4(1), 35–48.

Chaudhary, A., Kaushik, K., & Kumar, S. (2023). Blockchain from a modern perspective: An evolution to health science. In Chernyshenko, V. & Mkrttchian, V. (Eds.), *Blockchain Applications-Transforming Industries, Enhancing Security, and Addressing Ethical Considerations* (p. 87). IntechOpen.

Chaudhuri, R., Chatterjee, S., & Vrontis, D. (2024). Adoption of blockchain technology in hospitality and tourism industry and sustainability performance: Impact of technological turbulence and senior leadership support. *EuroMed Journal of Business*, 19(1), 62–83.

Chen, H. A., Clarke, N., & Lin, K. J. (2024). Blockchain and earnings management: Evidence from the supply chain. *British Accounting Review*, Forthcoming.

Chen, R., Li, Y., Yu, Y., Li, H., Chen, X., & Susilo, W. (2020). Blockchain-based dynamic provable data possession for smart cities. *IEEE Internet of Things Journal*, 7(5), 4143–4154.

Chen, T. Y., Huang, W. N., Kuo, P. C., Chung, H., & Chao, T. W. (2018). DEXON: A highly scalable, decentralized DAG-based consensus algorithm. *arXiv preprint arXiv:1811.07525*.

Chen, X., Cheng, Q., & Luo, T. (2024). The economic value of blockchain applications: Early evidence from asset-backed securities. *Management Science*, 70(1), 439–463.

Chen, Y., Lu, Y., Bulysheva, L., & Kataev, M. Y. (2022). Applications of blockchain in industry 4.0: A review. *Information Systems Frontiers*, 26(3), 1–15.

Chin, T., Wang, W., Yang, M., Duan, Y., & Chen, Y. (2021). The moderating effect of managerial discretion on blockchain technology and the firms' innovation quality: Evidence from Chinese manufacturing firms. *International Journal of Production Economics*, 240, 108219.

References   153

Choobineh, M., Arab, A., Khodaei, A., & Paaso, A. (2022). Energy innovations through blockchain: Challenges, opportunities, and the road ahead. *The Electricity Journal, 35*(1), 107059.

Clark, A., & Mihailov, A. (2019). Why private cryptocurrencies cannot serve as international reserves but central bank digital currencies can. University of Reading–Department of Economics Discussion Paper Series, 2019-09.

Clark, P. (2010). *The 15 Business Benefits of a Loyalty Initiative.* The Wise Marketer.

Clark, S., MacLachlan, M., Marshall, K., Morahan, N., Carroll, C., Hand, K., ... & O'Sullivan, K. (2022). Including digital connection in the United Nations sustainable development goals: A systems thinking approach for achieving the SDGs. *Sustainability, 14*(3), 1883.

Cohn, A., West, T., & Parker, C. (2016). Smart after all: Blockchain, smart contracts, parametric insurance, and smart energy grids. *Georgetown Law Technology Review, 1*, 273.

Coinchek (2023). Coincheck – Exploring Some Key Facts About the Coincheck Exchange. https://coincheck.com/

Dadkhah, M., Rahimnia, F., & Filimonau, V. (2022). Evaluating the opportunities, challenges and risks of applying the blockchain technology in tourism: A Delphi study approach. *Journal of Hospitality and Tourism Technology, 13*(5), 922–954.

Dalal, J. (2021). The amalgamation of blockchain and IoT: A survey. In *Proceedings of Second International Conference on Computing, Communications, and Cyber-Security: IC4S 2020* (pp. 775–786). Springer Singapore.

Davidson, S., De Filippi, P., & Potts, J. (2016). Economics of blockchain. *Decision Support Systems, 62*, 54–65. Available at SSRN 2744751.

De Filippi, P., & Loveluck, B. (2016). The invisible politics of Bitcoin: Governance crisis of a decentralized infrastructure. *Internet Policy Review, 5*(4), 32.

De Vries, A., & Stoll, C. (2021). Bitcoin's growing e-waste problem. *Resources, Conservation and Recycling, 175*, 105901.

Dierksmeier, C., & Seele, P. (2020). Blockchain and business ethics. *Business Ethics: A European Review, 29*(2), 348–359.

Ding, Y., & Sato, H. (2020, July). Dagbase: A decentralized database platform using DAG-based consensus. In *2020 IEEE 44th Annual Computers, Software, and Applications Conference (COMPSAC)* (pp. 798–807). IEEE.

Disparte, D. (2019). Why enterprise blockchain projects fail. *Forbes Magazine.*

Dogru, T., Mody, M., & Leonardi, C. (2018). *Blockchain Technology & Its Implications for the Hospitality Industry.* Boston University, 1–12.

Dowling, G. R., & Uncles, M. (1997). Do customer loyalty programs really work?. *Sloan Management Review, 38*, 71–82.

154 References

Dreyfuss (2021). American Airlines, travel platform Winding Tree announce blockchain partnership. www.reuters.com/business/finance/american-airlines-travel-platform-winding-tree-announce-blockchain-partnership-2021-11-16/

Dudin, M. N., & Kononova, E. V. (2020). Digitalization of university management in Russia and foreign countries as a necessary measure to ensure their economic security. *Market Economy Problems*, *3*, 95.

Duncan, G. (2022). Motion planning and remote sensing algorithms, predictive geospatial modeling and deep learning artificial intelligence tools, and machine perception and image recognition technologies in the blockchain-based virtual economy. *Analysis and Metaphysics*, *21*, 193–209.

Dutta, P., Choi, T. M., Somani, S., & Butala, R. (2020). Blockchain technology in supply chain operations: Applications, challenges and research opportunities. *Transportation Research Part E: Logistics and Transportation Review*, *142*, 102067.

Edastama, P., Purnama, S., Widayanti, R., Meria, L., & Rivelino, D. (2021). The potential blockchain technology in higher education learning innovations in era 4.0. *Blockchain Frontier Technology*, *1*(1), 104–113.

Ehret, M., & Wirtz, J. (2017). Unlocking value from machines: Business models and the industrial internet of things. *Journal of Marketing Management*, *33*(1–2), 111–130.

Ehret, M., & Wirtz, J. (2022). Contract innovation: Driving scale and scope of nonownership value propositions—Chapter description. In *The Palgrave Handbook of Service Management* (pp. 247–261). Springer International Publishing.

El Koshiry, A., Eliwa, E., Abd El-Hafeez, T., & Shams, M. Y. (2023). Unlocking the power of blockchain in education: An overview of innovations and outcomes. *Blockchain: Research and Applications*, *4*(4), P1–19, 100165.

Erceg, A., Damoska Sekuloska, J., & Kelić, I. (2020, February). Blockchain in the tourism industry—A review of the situation in Croatia and Macedonia. In *Informatics* (Vol. 7, No. (1), p. 5). MDPI.

Erol, I., Neuhofer, I. O., Dogru, T., Oztel, A., Searcy, C., & Yorulmaz, A. C. (2022). Improving sustainability in the tourism industry through blockchain technology: Challenges and opportunities. *Tourism Management*, *93*, 104628.

European Commission (2022). European Declaration on Digital Rights and Principles for the Digital Decade. https://eur-lex.europa.eu/legal-content/EN/TXT/PDF/?uri=CELEX:52022DC0028

European Commission (2023). Blockchain Strategy. https://digital-strategy.ec.europa.eu/en/policies/blockchain-strategy

Fahmi, N., Hastasakti, D. E., Zaspiagi, D., Saputra, R. K., & Wijayanti, S. (2023). A comparison of blockchain application and security issues from Bitcoin to cybersecurity. *Blockchain Frontier Technology*, *2*(2), 58–65.

References   155

Fedorova, E. P., & Skobleva, E. I. (2020). Application of blockchain technology in higher education. *European Journal of Contemporary Education, 9*(3), 552–571.

Filimonau, V., & Naumova, E. (2020). The blockchain technology and the scope of its application in hospitality operations. *International Journal of Hospitality Management, 87,* 102383.

Fischer, D. (2018). Ethical and professional implications of blockchain accounting ledgers. *Proceedings of the Northeast Business & Economics Association* (pp. 27–30). http://dx.doi.org/10.2139/ssrn.3331009.

Fragnière, E., Sahut, J. M., Hikkerova, L., Schegg, R., Schumacher, M., Grèzes, S., & Ramseyer, R. (2022). Blockchain technology in the tourism industry: New perspectives in Switzerland. *Journal of Innovation Economics Management, 37*(1), 65–90.

French, A., Shim, J. P., Risius, M., Larsen, K. R., & Jain, H. (2021). The 4th Industrial Revolution powered by the integration of AI, blockchain, and 5G. *Communications of the Association for Information Systems, 49*(1), 6.

Gai, K., Hu, Z., Zhu, L., Wang, R., & Zhang, Z. (2020). Blockchain meets DAG: A BlockDAG consensus mechanism. In *Algorithms and Architectures for Parallel Processing: 20th International Conference*, ICA3PP 2020, New York City, NY, USA, October 2–4, 2020, Proceedings, Part III (pp. 110–125). Springer International Publishing.

Garcia, P. (2018). Biometrics on the blockchain. *Biometric Technology Today, 2018*(5), 5–7.

García, R., Cediel, A., Teixidó, M., & Gil, R. (2021, September). Copyrightly: Blockchain and semantic web for decentralised copyright management. In *International Conference on the Economics of Grids, Clouds, Systems, and Services* (pp. 199–206). Springer International Publishing.

Garcia-Garcia, J. A., Sánchez-Gómez, N., Lizcano, D., Escalona, M. J., & Wojdyński, T. (2020). Using blockchain to improve collaborative business process management: Systematic literature review. *IEEE Access, 8,* 142312–142336.

Garcia-Teruel, R. M. (2020). Legal challenges and opportunities of blockchain technology in the real estate sector. *Journal of Property, Planning and Environmental Law, 12*(2), 129–145.

Gillis, S. (2023). Blockchain-based Application for Insurance Claims Management Master's thesis, Harvard University.

González-Mendes, S., González-Sánchez, R., Costa, C. J., & García-Muiña, F. (2023, June). Analysing the state of the art of Blockchain application in smart cities: A bibliometric study. *In 2023 18th Iberian Conference on Information Systems and Technologies (CISTI)* (pp. 1–6). IEEE.

Gorniak-Kocikowska, K. (1996). The computer revolution and the problem of global ethics. *Science and Engineering Ethics, 2,* 177–190.

156 References

Gössling, S. (2021). Tourism, technology and ICT: A critical review of affordances and concessions. *Journal of Sustainable Tourism, 29*(5), 733–750.

Goudarzi, H., & Martin, J. I. (2018). Blockchain in aviation. Retrieved from International Air Transport Association website: www. iata. org/contentassets/2d997082f3c84c7cba001f506edd2c2e/blockchain-in-aviation-white-paper. pdf.

Grech, A., & Camilleri, A. F. (2017). *Blockchain in education.* Publications Office of the European Union.

Griffin, J., & Lowenstein, M. W. (2002). *Customer winback: How to recapture lost customers – And keep them loyal.* John Wiley.

Grzyb (2023). Deep Dive Into FATF – The World's Biggest Crypto Opponent. www.linkedin.com/pulse/deep-dive-fatf-worlds-biggest-crypto-opponent-wiktor-grzyb/

Gültekin, Y. (2017). Cryptocurrencies as an alternative medium of payment in tourism industry: Bitcoin, 96–113.

Gupta, C. P., & Patel, A. R. (2022, August). Scope and challenges of blockchain in Indian supply chain transformation for MSMEs. In *2022 International Conference on Emerging Techniques in Computational Intelligence (ICETCI)* (pp. 115–120). IEEE.

Gupta, R., Shukla, V. K., Rao, S. S., Anwar, S., Sharma, P., & Bathla, R. (2020, January). Enhancing privacy through "smart contract" using blockchain-based dynamic access control. In 2020 *International Conference on Computation, Automation and Knowledge Management (ICCAKM)* (pp. 338–343). IEEE.

Gupta, S. S. (2017). Blockchain. IBM Online (www.IBM.COM).

Halkiopoulos, C., Antonopoulou, H., & Kostopoulos, N. (2023). Utilizing blockchain technology in various applications to secure data flows. A comprehensive analysis. *Technium, 11*(1), 44–55.

Han, P., Sui, A., Jiang, T., & Gu, C. (2020, August). Copyright certificate storage and trading system based on blockchain. In *2020 IEEE International Conference on Advances in Electrical Engineering and Computer Applications (AEECA)* (pp. 611–615). IEEE.

Handayani, I., Apriani, D., Mulyati, M., Yusuf, N. A., & Zahra, A. R. A. (2023). A survey on user experience of blockchain transactions: Security and adaptability issues. *Blockchain Frontier Technology, 3*(1), 80–88.

Hernandez, J., & Kiff, J. (2024). Evolving capital markets Part II: Exploring blockchain-based government bonds. Available at SSRN. http://dx.doi.org/10.2139/ssrn.4771943

Hill, N., & Brierley, J. (2017). *How to Measure Customer Satisfaction.* Routledge.

Hoffman, M. R., Ibáñez, L. D., & Simperl, E. (2020). Toward a formal scholarly understanding of blockchain-mediated decentralization: A systematic review and a framework. *Frontiers in Blockchain, 3*, 35.

References   157

HTNG. (2018). Blockchain for hospitality. Retrieved from Hospitality Technology Next Generation website: www.hospitalitynet.org/file/152008 497.pdf

Hua, X., Huang, Y., & Zheng, Y. (2019). Current practices, new insights, and emerging trends of financial technologies. *Industrial Management & Data Systems, 119*(7), 1401–1410.

Huertas, J., Liu, H., & Robinson, S. (2018). Eximchain: Supply Chain Finance solutions on a secured public, permissioned blockchain hybrid. Eximchain white paper, 13.

Hughes, A., Park, A., Kietzmann, J., & Archer-Brown, C. (2019). Beyond Bitcoin: What blockchain and distributed ledger technologies mean for firms. *Business Horizons, 62*(3), 273–281.

Huseynov, F., & Mitchell, J. (2024). Blockchain for environmental peacebuilding: Application in water management. *Digital Policy, Regulation and Governance, 26*(1), 55–71.

IATA (2018). Blockchain in aviation exploring the fundamentals, use cases, and industry initiatives. www.iata.org/contentassets/2d997082f3c84c7cb a001f506edd2c2e/blockchain-in-aviation-white-paper.pdf

Ingold, P. V., & Langer, M. (2021). Resume = Resume? The effects of blockchain, social media, and classical resumes on resume fraud and applicant reactions to resumes. *Computers in Human Behavior, 114*, 106573.

Irvin, C., & Sullivan, J. (2018). Using blockchain to streamline airline finance. Retrieved from Deloitte Development LLC website: www2. deloitte. com/ us/en/pages/consulting/articles/airlines-blockchain-finance. html, 1–6.

Islam, M. J., Rahman, A., Kabir, S., Karim, M. R., Acharjee, U. K., Nasir, M. K., ... & Wu, S. (2021). Blockchain-SDN-based energy-aware and distributed secure architecture for IoT in smart cities. *IEEE Internet of Things Journal, 9*(5), 3850–3864.

Ivaninskiy, I., & Ivashkovskaya, I. (2022). Are blockchain-based digital transformation and ecosystem-based business models mutually reinforcing? The principal-agent conflict perspective. *Eurasian Business Review, 12*(4), 643–670.

Ivanov, S. H., & Webster, C. (2017, June). The robot as a consumer: A research agenda. In *Marketing: Experience and Perspectives Conference* (pp. 29–30).

Jain, S., Sharma, C., Das, P., Shambhu, S., & Chen, H. Y. (2023). Blockchain and cryptocurrency: A bibliometric analysis. *Journal of Advanced Computational Intelligence and Intelligent Informatics, 27*(5), 822–836.

Jiang, Y., Tran, T. H., & Williams, L. (2023). A surveillance-and-blockchain-based tracking system for mitigation of baggage mishandling at smart airports. *Journal of Airline Operations and Aviation Management, 2*(2), 33–51.

Johng, H., Kim, D., Hill, T., & Chung, L. (2018, July). Using blockchain to enhance the trustworthiness of business processes: A goal-oriented

158   References

approach. In *2018 IEEE International Conference on Services Computing (SCC)* (pp. 249–252). IEEE.

Johnson, D. (2019). Blockchain-based voting in the US and EU constitutional orders: A digital technology to secure democratic values?. *European Journal of Risk Regulation, 10*(2), 330–358.

Johnson, D., & Smith, J. (2023). Using a secure blockchain framework hospitals may manage their health insurance policies.

Johnson, L., Isam, A., Gogerty, N., & Zitoli, J. (2015, December 11). Connecting the blockchain to the sun to save the planet. Available at SSRN 2702639. http://dx.doi.org/10.2139/ssrn.2702639

Johnson, O. (2022, May). Decentralized reinsurance: Funding blockchain-based parametric bushfire insurance. In *2022 IEEE International Conference on Blockchain and Cryptocurrency (ICBC)* (pp. 1–3). IEEE.

Jones, C. B., & Kingsley, D. J. (2023). Decentralized blockchain with convolutional neural network model for security attack mitigation. *ICTACT Journal on Communication Technology, 14*(1), 2843.

Joshi, A. P., Han, M., & Wang, Y. (2018). A survey on security and privacy issues of blockchain technology. *Mathematical Foundations of Computing, 1*(2), 121–147.

Kannan, K., Singh, A., Verma, M., Jayachandran, P., & Mehta, S. (2020, November). Blockchain-based platform for trusted collaborations on data and AI models. In *2020 IEEE International Conference on Blockchain (Blockchain)* (pp. 82–89). IEEE.

Karame, G. O., & Androulaki, E. (2016). *Bitcoin and blockchain security.* Artech House.

Karinsalo, A., & Halunen, K. (2018, July). Smart contracts for a mobility-as-a-service ecosystem. In *2018 IEEE International Conference on Software Quality, Reliability and Security Companion (QRS-C)* (pp. 135–138). IEEE.

Kaye (2022). Insight: Australian stock exchange's blockchain failure burns market trust. www.reuters.com/markets/australian-stock-exchanges-blockchain-failure-burns-market-trust-2022-12-20/

Kim, J. W. (2020). Blockchain technology and its applications: Case studies. *Journal of System and Management Sciences, 10*(1), 83–93.

Kim, J., & Duffy, V. G. (2022). A systematic literature review of the emergence of blockchain technology in of human resources management. In Duffy, V.G., Lehto, M., Yih, Y., & Proctor, R.W. (Eds.), *Human-Automation Interaction: Manufacturing, Services and User Experience* (Vol. 10, pp. 109–122). Springer. https://doi.org/10.1007/978-3-031-10780-1_6

Kirkwood, J. W. (2022). From work to proof of work: Meaning and value after blockchain. *Critical Inquiry, 48*(2), 360–380.

Kizildag, M., Dogru, T., Zhang, T. C., Mody, M. A., Altin, M., Ozturk, A. B., & Ozdemir, O. (2019). Blockchain: A paradigm shift in business practices.

References 159

International Journal of Contemporary Hospitality Management, 32(3), 953–975.

Köhler, S., Bager, S., & Pizzol, M. (2022). Sustainability standards and blockchain in agro-food supply chains: Synergies and conflicts. *Technological Forecasting and Social Change, 185*, 122094.

Korpela, K., Hallikas, J., & Dahlberg, T. (2017). Digital supply chain transformation toward blockchain integration. *Proceedings of the 50th Hawaii International Conference on System Sciences.*

Kowalewski, D., McLaughlin, J., & Hill, A. J. (2017). Blockchain will transform customer loyalty programs. *Harvard Business Review, 14*, 1–12.

Kowalewski, D., & Simon, G. (2016). Will blockchain technology rewrite loyalty?, Hotel News Now.

Krishna (2021). Equifax Hack: 5 Biggest Credit Card Data Breaches. www. investopedia.com/news/5-biggest-credit-card-data-hacks-history/

Kshetri, N. (2017). Can blockchain strengthen the internet of things?. *IT Professional, 19*(4), 68–72.

Kshetri, N. (2018). Blockchain and electronic healthcare records [cybertrust]. *Computer, 51*(12), 59–63.

Kučera, J., & Bruckner, T. (2019). Blockchain and ethics: A brief overview of the emerging initiatives. In *BIR Workshops BIR Workshops* (Vol. 2443, pp. 129–139).

Kwok, A. O., & Koh, S. G. (2019). Is blockchain technology a watershed for tourism development? *Current Issues in Tourism, 22*(20), 2447–2452.

Lapointe, C., & Fishbane, L. (2019). The blockchain ethical design framework. *Innovations: Technology, Governance, Globalization, 12*(3–4), 50–71.

Larchet, V. (2017). Blockchain: Solution for the black market threat to the tourism industry. Retrieved from SecuTix website: www. secutix. com/wp-content/uploads/2017/07/White-paper_Blockchain_final. pdf, 1–14.

Lee, K. L., & Zhang, T. (2023). Revolutionizing supply chains: Unveiling the power of blockchain technology for enhanced transparency and performance. *International Journal of Technology, Innovation and Management (IJTIM), 3*(1), 19–27.

Leible, S., Schlager, S., Schubotz, M., & Gipp, B. (2019). A review on blockchain technology and blockchain projects fostering open science. *Frontiers in Blockchain, 2*, 486595.

Lewis, M. (2004). The influence of loyalty programs and short-term promotions on customer retention. *Journal of Marketing Research, 41*(3), 281–292.

Lewis, R., McPartland, J., & Ranjan, R. (2017). Blockchain and financial market innovation. *Economic Perspectives, 41*(7), 1–17.

Li, H., Xiao, F., Yin, L., & Wu, F. (2021). Application of blockchain technology in energy trading: A review. *Frontiers in Energy Research, 9*, 671133.

160 References

Liang, W., Tang, M., Long, J., Peng, X., Xu, J., & Li, K. C. (2019). A secure fabric blockchain-based data transmission technique for industrial Internet-of-Things. *IEEE Transactions on Industrial Informatics, 15*(6), 3582–3592.

Lin, Y. P., Petway, J. R., Anthony, J., Mukhtar, H., Liao, S. W., Chou, C. F., & Ho, Y. F. (2017). Blockchain: The evolutionary next step for ICT e-agriculture. *Environments, 4*(3), 50.

Liu, H., Jiang, N., Ortiz, G. G. R., Cong, P. T., Phuong, T. T. T., & Wisetsri, W. (2023). Exploring tourism business model importance with the emergence of blockchain system: Directions for tourism industry of China. *Environmental Science and Pollution Research, 30*(16), 46647–46656.

Lohachab, A. (2021). A perspective on using blockchain for ensuring security in smart card systems. In *Research Anthology on Blockchain Technology in Business, Healthcare, Education, and Government* (pp. 529–558). IGI Global.

Lohmer, J., & Lasch, R. (2020). Blockchain in operations management and manufacturing: Potential and barriers. *Computers & Industrial Engineering, 149*, 106789.

Lowenstein, M. (2002). *Customer Win back – The 15 business benefits of a loyalty initiative.* John Wiley.

Lu, Q., & Xu, X. (2017). Adaptable blockchain-based systems: A case study for product traceability. *IEEE Software, 34*(6), 21–27.

Lubowiecki-Vikuk, A., Budzanowska-Drzewiecka, M., Borzyszkowski, J., & Taheri, B. (2023). Critical reflection on VUCA in tourism and hospitality marketing activities. *International Journal of Contemporary Hospitality Management, 35*(8), 2983–3005.

Ludeiro, A. R. (2019). Blockchain technology for luggage tracking. In *Distributed Computing and Artificial Intelligence*, Special Sessions, 15th International Conference (pp. 451–456). Springer International Publishing.

Lutfiani, N., Apriani, D., Nabila, E. A., & Juniar, H. L. (2022). Academic certificate fraud detection system framework using blockchain technology. *Blockchain Frontier Technology, 1*(2), 55–64.

Maythu, Y., Kwok, A. O., & Teh, P. L. (2024). Blockchain technology diffusion in tourism: Evidence from early enterprise adopters and innovators. *Heliyon, 10*(2), e24675.

Melnychenko, S., Mazaraki, N., & Tkachuk, T. (2019, May). Leading trends in tourism: Blockchain in franchising. In *3rd International Conference on Social, Economic, and Academic Leadership (ICSEAL 2019)* (pp. 388–395). Atlantis Press.

Mileti, A., Arduini, D., Watson, G., & Giangrande, A. (2022). Blockchain traceability in trading biomasses obtained with an integrated multi-trophic aquaculture. *Sustainability, 15*(1), 767.

Miller, D. (2018). Blockchain and the internet of things in the industrial sector. *IT Professional, 20*(3), 15–18.

References 161

Miller, M., Williams, S., Dagher, G. G., & Long, M. (2023, November). PRISM: A blockchain-enabled reputation-based consensus for enhancing scientific workflow provenance. In *2023 IEEE 9th International Conference on Collaboration and Internet Computing (CIC)* (pp. 72–81). IEEE.

Mittelstadt, B. D., Allo, P., Taddeo, M., Wachter, S., & Floridi, L. (2016). The ethics of algorithms: Mapping the debate. *Big Data & Society, 3*(2), 2053951716679679.

Mohan, T. (2018). Improve food supply chain traceability using blockchain. Thesis dissertation. Penn State University Libraries.

Mougayar, W. (2016). *The Business Blockchain: Promise, Practice, and Application of the Next Internet Technology*. John Wiley.

Mucchi, L., Milanesi, M., & Becagli, C. (2022). Blockchain technologies for museum management. The case of the loan of cultural objects. *Current Issues in Tourism, 25*(18), 3042–3056.

Muir, M. (2023). Miners seek financial lifeline amid bitcoin price recovery; Crypto. Soaring tokens Upsurge in warehouse activity signals that battered sector might be crawling back to life. *The Financial Times*, 8.

Mujačević, E. (2024). Application of cryptocurrency as a method of payment in tourism. *Tourism and Hospitality Management, 30*(1), 39–49.

Nagel, E., & Kranz, J. (2020). Exploring Technological Artefacts at the 'Trust Frontier' of Blockchain Token Sales. European Conference on Information System – Marrakech. https://web.archive.org/web/20210813001235 id_/https://aisel.aisnet.org/cgi/viewcontent.cgi?article=1117&context=ecis 2020_rp

Nam, J., & Choi, M. (2022). IoT edge cloud platform with revocatable blockchain smart contract. *Journal of Logistics, Informatics and Service Science, 9*(2), 131–144.

Negi, D., Sah, A., Rawat, S., Choudhury, T., & Khanna, A. (2021). Block chain platforms and smart contracts. In *Blockchain Applications in IoT Ecosystem* (pp. 65–76). Springer International Publishing.

Nikitina, A. A., & Tishchenko, S. V. (2018). Blockchain technologies are an innovative breakthrough in tourism. *Problems of Economics and Legal Practice, 2*, 218–220.

Nuryyev, G., Spyridou, A., Yeh, S., & Lo, C. C. (2021). Factors of digital payment adoption in hospitality businesses: A conceptual approach. *European Journal of Tourism Research, 29*, 2905.

Nuryyev, G., Wang, Y. P., Achyldurdyyeva, J., Jaw, B. S., Yeh, Y. S., Lin, H. T., & Wu, L. F. (2020). Blockchain technology adoption behavior and sustainability of the business in tourism and hospitality SMEs: An empirical study. *Sustainability, 12*(3), 1256.

Obim, I. E., Ukwueze, P. O., & Nwadike, C. (2023). Utilization of blockchain technology for effective circulation control in university libraries in

162 References

South-East, Nigeria. *Information Impact: Journal of Information and Knowledge Management, 14*(2), 1–15.

Ovezik, C., Karakostas, D., & Kiayias, A. (2024). SoK: A stratified approach to blockchain decentralization. In *Financial Cryptography and Data Security 2024: Twenty-Eighth International Conference* (pp. 1632–1643). Springer.

Owraigbo, L. (2023). Awareness and application of blockchain technology among librarians for effective service delivery in university libraries in South-South, Nigeria. *Library Philosophy and Practice*, 1–17.

Ozdemir, A. I., Ar, I. M., & Erol, I. (2020). Assessment of blockchain applications in travel and tourism industry. *Quality & Quantity, 54*, 1549–1563.

Özgit, H., & Adalıer, A. (2022). Can Blockchain technology help small islands achieve sustainable tourism? A perspective on North Cyprus. *Worldwide Hospitality and Tourism Themes, 14*(4), 374–383.

Palas, M. J. U., & Bunduchi, R. (2020). Exploring interpretations of blockchain's value in healthcare: A multi-stakeholder approach. *Information Technology & People, 34*(2), 453–495.

Panina, E., Simbuletova, R., & Kakhuzheva, Z. (2022). Analysis of the applicability of blockchain technology in tourism. In *SHS Web of Conferences SHS Web of Conferences* (Vol. 141, p. 0100701007). EDP Sciences.

Park, A., Wilson, M., Robson, K., Demetis, D., & Kietzmann, J. (2023). Interoperability: Our exciting and terrifying Web3 future. *Business Horizons, 66*(4), 529–541.

Passerat-Palmbach, J., Farnan, T., Miller, R., Gross, M. S., Flannery, H. L., & Gleim, B. (2019). A blockchain-orchestrated federated learning architecture for healthcare consortia. arXiv preprint arXiv:1910.12603.

Patel, R., Migliavacca, M., & Oriani, M. E. (2022). Blockchain in banking and finance: A bibliometric review. *Research in International Business and Finance, 62*, 101718.

Pilkington, M. (2016). Blockchain technology: Principles and applications. In Olleros, F. X. & Zhegu, M. (Eds.), *Research Handbook on Digital Transformations* (pp. 225–253). Edward Elgar Publishing.

Pilkington, M. (2017). Bitcoin through the lenses of complexity theory. In Pollard, J. & Martin, R. (Eds.), *Handbook on the Geographies of Money and Finance* (pp. 610–636). Edward Elgar Publishing.

Pilkington, M. (2020). The relation between tokens and blockchain networks: The case of medical tourism in the Republic of Moldova. *The Journal of the British Blockchain Association.* https://doi.org/10.31585/jbba-4-1-(2)2021

Portnoff, R. S., Huang, D. Y., Doerfler, P., Afroz, S., & McCoy, D. (2017, August). Backpage and Bitcoin: Uncovering human traffickers. In *Proceedings of the 23rd ACM SIGKDD International Conference on*

References   163

Knowledge Discovery and Data Mining,Halifax, NS, Canada (pp. 1595–1604).

Pradhan, N. R., & Singh, A. P. (2021). Smart contracts for automated control system in blockchain based smart cities. *Journal of Ambient Intelligence and Smart Environments*, *13*(3), 253–267.

Prados-Castillo, J. F., Torrecilla-García, J. A., Andraz, G., & Guaita Martínez, J. M. (2023). Blockchain in peer-to-peer platforms: Enhancing sustainability and customer experience in tourism. *Sustainability*, *15*(22), 15968.

Pranita, D., Sarjana, S., Musthofa, B. M., Kusumastuti, H., & Rasul, M. S. (2023). Blockchain technology to enhance integrated blue economy: A case study in strengthening sustainable tourism on smart islands. *Sustainability*, *15*(6), 5342.

Quan, Y., Wu, X., Deng, W., & Zhang, L. (2023). Decoding social sentiment in DAO: A comparative analysis of blockchain governance communities. arXiv preprint arXiv:2311.14676.

Radic, A., Quan, W., Koo, B., Chua, B. L., Kim, J. J., & Han, H. (2022). Central bank digital currency as a payment method for tourists: Application of the theory of planned behavior to digital Yuan/Won/Dollar choice. *Journal of Travel & Tourism Marketing*, *39*(2), 152–172.

Rajasekaran, A. S., Azees, M., & Al-Turjman, F. (2022). A comprehensive survey on blockchain technology. *Sustainable Energy Technologies and Assessments*, *52*, 102039.

Ramadhan, T., Wahid, W. N., Nusantoro, H., & Rifki, A. (2022). New authoritative changes with blockchain an emphasis production network. *Blockchain Frontier Technology*, *2*(1), 24–35.

Rana, R. L., Adamashvili, N., & Tricase, C. (2022). The impact of blockchain technology adoption on tourism industry: A systematic literature review. *Sustainability*, *14*(12), 7383.

Ratna, S., Saide, S., Putri, A. M., Indrajit, R. E., & Muwardi, D. (2024). Digital transformation in tourism and hospitality industry: A literature review of blockchain, financial technology, and knowledge management. *EuroMed Journal of Business*, *19*(1), 84–112.

Reddy, S., & Sharma, G. V. V. (2020, November). UL-blockDAG: Unsupervised learning based consensus protocol for blockchain. In *2020 IEEE 40th International Conference on Distributed Computing Systems (ICDCS)* (pp. 1243–1248). IEEE.

Research and Markets (2023) "Global Travel Technologies Business Analysis Report 2023: Market to Reach $10.7 Billion by 2030 – Blockchain Technology to Radically Transform Travel Industry" www.globenewswire. com/news-release/2023/11/29/2787627/0/en/Global-Travel-Technologies-Business-Analysis-Report-2023-Market-to-Reach-10-7-Billion-by-2030-Blockchain-Technology-to-Radically-Transform-Travel-Industry.html

164 *References*

Riechmann, J. M. (2020). Blockchain takes to the skies: An assessment of blockchain applications in the airline industry (Doctoral dissertation).

Rodrigo, M. N. N., Perera, S., Senaratne, S., & Jin, X. (2020). Potential application of blockchain technology for embodied carbon estimating in construction supply chains. *Buildings, 10*(8), 140.

Ross, E. S. (2017). Nobody puts blockchain in a corner: The disruptive role of blockchain technology in the financial services industry and current regulatory issues. *Catholic University Journal of Law and Technology, 25*(2), 7.

Rugeviciute, A., & Mehrpouya, A. (2019). Blockchain, a panacea for development accountability? A study of the barriers and enablers for blockchain's adoption by development aid organizations. *Frontiers in Blockchain, 2*, 15.

Sankar, J. G., & David, A. (2024). Transforming the travel landscape: Smart contracts in tourism management. In *Decentralizing the Online Experience With Web3 Technologies*, (pp. 246–266). IGI Global.

Santos, J., & Duffy, K. H. (2022). A decentralized approach to blockcerts certificate revocation. Available online: https://github.com/WebOfTrustInfo/rwot5-boston/tree/master/final-documents

Saulina, A., & Delhi, A. (2024). Implementation of the public blockchain technology system in the future to increase tourist visits in Tangerang City. *Blockchain Frontier Technology, 3*(2), 132–137.

Schatsky, D., & Muraskin, C. (2015). Beyond Bitcoin. Blockchain is coming to disrupt your industry, Deloitte Insight, 7.

Sharma, M., Sehrawat, R., Daim, T., & Shaygan, A. (2021). Technology assessment: Enabling Blockchain in hospitality and tourism sectors. *Technological Forecasting and Social Change, 169*, 120810.

Shin, D. D. (2019). Blockchain: The emerging technology of digital trust. *Telematics and Informatics, 45*, 101278.

Shin, D., & Ibahrine, M. (2020). The socio-technical assemblages of blockchain system: How blockchains are framed and how the framing reflects societal contexts. *Digital Policy, Regulation and Governance, 22*(3), 245–263.

Shrestha, R., & Nam, S. Y. (2019). Regional blockchain for vehicular networks to prevent 51% attacks. *IEEE Access, 7*, 95033–95045.

Sigala, M. (2018). New technologies in tourism: From multi-disciplinary to anti-disciplinary advances and trajectories. *Tourism Management Perspectives, 25*, 151–155.

Singh, A., Kumar, G., Saha, R., Conti, M., Alazab, M., & Thomas, R. (2022). A survey and taxonomy of consensus protocols for blockchains. *Journal of Systems Architecture, 127*, 102503.

Singh, S., Rajput, N. K., Rathi, V. K., Pandey, H. M., Jaiswal, A. K., & Tiwari, P. (2020). Securing blockchain transactions using quantum teleportation and quantum digital signature. *Neural Processing Letters, 55*(4), 3827–3842.

References   165

Smith, S. S. (2021). Decentralized finance & accounting-implications, considerations, and opportunities for development. *International Journal of Digital Accounting Research, 21,* 129–153.

Soana, G. (2024). The Anti Money Laundering Regulation of Crypto-Assets in Europe: A Critical Analysis. Doctoral thesis. https://iris.luiss.it/handle/11385/238740.

Sokołowski, A., Wrzalik, A., & Niedbał, R. (2023). Blockchain technology awareness among managers of large enterprise. *Procedia Computer Science, 225,* 3031–3039.

Sompolinsky, Y., Lewenberg, Y., & Zohar, A. (2016). Spectre: Serialization of proof-of-work events: Confirming transactions via recursive elections. hNps. eprint. iacr. org/2016/1159. pdf

Sompolinsky, Y., Wyborski, S., & Zohar, A. (2021, September). Phantom Ghostdag: A scalable generalization of Nakamoto consensus: September 2, 2021. In *Proceedings of the 3rd ACM Conference on Advances in Financial Technologies,* New York (pp. 57–70). Association for Computing Machinery.

Sonkor, M. S., & Dde Soto, B. G. (2022, February). Towards secure construction networks: A data-sharing architecture utilizing blockchain technology and decentralized storage. In *Proceedings Construction Blockchain Consortium Conference,* London, UK (pp. 20–22).

Spychiger, F., Tasca, P., & Tessone, C. J. (2021). Unveiling the importance and evolution of design components through the "tree of blockchain". *Frontiers in Blockchain, 3,* 613476.

Srivastava, G., Parizi, R. M., & Dehghantanha, A. (2020). The future of blockchain technology in healthcare internet of things security. *Blockchain Cybersecurity, Trust and Privacy, 79,* 161.

Stein, B., Kuznecov, K., Lee, S., & Müller, J. (2018). A public blockchain solution permitting secure storage and deletion of private data—Draft. Lition Foundation, Berlin, Germany, Tech. Rep.

Sun, X., Yu, F. R., Zhang, P., Sun, Z., Xie, W., & Peng, X. (2021). A survey on zero-knowledge proof in blockchain. *IEEE Network, 35*(4), 198–205.

Sun Yin, H. H., Langenheldt, K., Harlev, M., Mukkamala, R. R., & Vatrapu, R. (2019). Regulating cryptocurrencies: A supervised machine learning approach to de-anonymizing the bitcoin blockchain. *Journal of Management Information Systems, 36*(1), 37–73.

Swan, M. (2015). Blockchain thinking: The brain as a decentralized autonomous corporation [commentary]. *IEEE Technology and Society Magazine, 34*(4), 41–52.

Takale, D. G., Damke, S., Mehra, S., Burkule, S., & Tadge, N (2024). Applications of blockchain in tourism industry. *Journal of Communication Engineering and VLSI Design, 2*(1), 8–15. https://doi.org/10.48001/JoCEVD

166 References

Tang, Y., Xiong, J., Becerril-Arreola, R., & Iyer, L. (2019, June). Blockchain ethics research: A conceptual model. In *Proceedings of the 2019 on Computers and People Research Conference*, New York (pp. 43–49).

Tapscott, D., & Tapscott, A. (2016). *Blockchain revolution: How the technology behind Bitcoin is changing money, business, and the world*. Penguin.

Thakur, A. (2022). A comprehensive study of the trends and analysis of distributed ledger technology and blockchain technology in the healthcare industry. *Frontiers in Blockchain, 5*, 844834.

Thakur, V., Doja, M. N., Dwivedi, Y. K., Ahmad, T., & Khadanga, G. (2020). Land records on blockchain for implementation of land titling in India. *International Journal of Information Management, 52*, 101940.

Tham, A., & Sigala, M. (2020). Road block (chain): Bit (coin)s for tourism sustainable development goals?. *Journal of Hospitality and Tourism Technology, 11*(2), 203–222.

Thees, H., Erschbamer, G., & Pechlaner, H. (2020). The application of blockchain in tourism: Use cases in the tourism value system. *European Journal of Tourism Research, 26*, 2602.

Tian, F. (2016, June). An agri-food supply chain traceability system for China based on RFID & blockchain technology. In *2016 13th International Conference on Service Systems and Service Management (ICSSSM)* (pp. 1–6). IEEE.

Tian, F. (2017, June). A supply chain traceability system for food safety based on HACCP, blockchain & Internet of things. In *2017 International Conference on Service Systems and Service Management* (pp. 1–6). IEEE.

Toufaily, E., Zalan, T., & Dhaou, S. B. (2021). A framework of blockchain technology adoption: An investigation of challenges and expected value. *Information & Management, 58*(3), 103444.

Treiblmaier, H. (2022). Blockchain and tourism. In Xiang, Z., Fuchs, M., Gretzel, U., & Höpken, W. (Eds.), *Handbook of e-Tourism* (pp. 475–495). Springer International Publishing.

Treiblmaier, H., & Önder, I. (2019). The impact of blockchain on the tourism industry: A theory-based research framework. In Treiblmaier, H. & Beck, R. (Eds.), *Business Transformation through Blockchain: Volume II* (pp. 3–21). Springer.

Treiblmaier, H., Rejeb, A., & Strebinger, A. (2020). Blockchain as a driver for smart city development: Application fields and a comprehensive research agenda. *Smart Cities, 3*(3), 853–872.

Treiblmaier, H., & Sillaber, C. (2021). The impact of blockchain on e-commerce: A framework for salient research topics. *Electronic Commerce Research and Applications, 48*, 101054.

Truby, J., Brown, R. D., Dahdal, A., & Ibrahim, I. (2022). Blockchain, climate damage, and death: Policy interventions to reduce the carbon emissions,

References 167

mortality, and net-zero implications of non-fungible tokens and Bitcoin. *Energy Research & Social Science, 88,* 102499.

TUI Group (2016). TUI to use blockchain opportunities. www.tuigroup.com/en-en/media/stories/special-themed-section/digitalisation-and-innovation/2017-06-22-tui-to-use-blockchain-opportunities

Turilli, M., & Floridi, L. (2009). The ethics of information transparency. *Ethics and Information Technology, 11,* 105–112.

Tyan, I., Yagüe, M. I., & Guevara-Plaza, A. (2021). Blockchain technology's potential for sustainable tourism. In *Information and Communication Technologies in Tourism 2021: Proceedings of the ENTER 2021 eTourism Conference,* January 19–22, 2021 (pp. 17–29). Springer International Publishing.

UNWTO, U. (2019). International tourism highlights. World Tourism. www.e-unwto.org/doi/pdf/10.18111/9789284421152

Valeri, M. (2020). Blockchain technology: Adoption perspectives in tourism. In Ratten, V. (Ed.), *Entrepreneurship and Organizational Change: Managing Innovation and Creative Capabilities* (pp. 27–35). Springer. https://doi.org/10.1007/978-3-030-35415-2_3

Van Nguyen, T., Cong Pham, H., Nhat Nguyen, M., Zhou, L., & Akbari, M. (2023). Data-driven review of blockchain applications in supply chain management: Key research themes and future directions. *International Journal of Production Research, 61*(23), 8213–8235.

Van Niekerk, A. J. (2024). Economic inclusion: Green finance and the SDGs. *Sustainability, 16*(3), 1128.

Vasani, V., Prateek, K., Amin, R., Maity, S., & Dwivedi, A. D. (2024). Embracing the quantum frontier: Investigating quantum communication, cryptography, applications and future directions. *Journal of Industrial Information Integration, 39,* 100594.

Wamba, S. F., Queiroz, M. M., Roscoe, S., Phillips, W., Kapletia, D., & Azadegan, A. (2021). Guest editorial: Emerging technologies in emergency situations. *International Journal of Operations & Production Management, 41*(9), 1405–1416.

Wang, Q., Li, R., & Zhan, L. (2021). Blockchain technology in the energy sector: From basic research to real world applications. *Computer Science Review, 39,* 100362.

Wang, X., Feng, L., Zhang, H., Lyu, C., Wang, L., & You, Y. (2017, April). Human resource information management model based on blockchain technology. In *2017 IEEE Symposium on Service-Oriented System Engineering (SOSE)* (pp. 168–173). IEEE.

Wang, X., Yang, W., Noor, S., Chen, C., Guo, M., & Van Dam, K. H. (2019). Blockchain-based smart contract for energy demand management. *Energy Procedia, 158,* 2719–2724.

168 References

Wang, Z. J., Chen, Z. S., Xiao, L., Su, Q., Govindan, K., & Skibniewski, M. J. (2023). Blockchain adoption in sustainable supply chains for Industry 5.0: A multistakeholder perspective. *Journal of Innovation & Knowledge*, 8(4), 100425.

Watkins, E. (2017). The Definitive Guide to Hotel Blockchain Technology. Retrieved December 10, 2017, from http://duettocloud.com/definitive-guide-hotel-blockchain-technology/

Watters, C. (2023). When criminals abuse the blockchain: Establishing personal jurisdiction in a decentralised environment. *Laws*, 12(2), 33.

Webjet limited (2018). Webjet launches first working blockchain initiative in the hotel distribution industry. www.annualreports.com/HostedData/Annu alReportArchive/W/ASX_WEB_2018.pdf

Wegner, P. (1996). Interoperability. *ACM Computing Surveys (CSUR)*, 28(1), 285–287.

Wener, R., Manfred, K., & Wayne, H. D. (2004, August). The customer relationship management process: Its measurements and impact on performance. *Journal of Marketing Research*, 41(3), 293–305.

Widhiasthini, N. W., Subawa, N. S., Fong Emmerson, M., Yanti, N. K. W., Utami, M. S. M., Kusuma, P. S. A. J., ..., & Sudharma, K. J. A. (2024). Public regulation urgency in cryptocurrency based on administrative reform for Bali sustainable tourism. *Cogent Social Sciences*, 10(1), 2312657.

Wilkie, A., & Smith, S. S. (2021). Blockchain: Speed, efficiency, decreased costs, and technical challenges. In *The Emerald Handbook of Blockchain for Business* (pp. 157–170). Emerald Publishing Limited.

Willie, P. (2019). Can all sectors of the hospitality and tourism industry be influenced by the innovation of blockchain technology?. *Worldwide Hospitality and Tourism Themes*, 11(2), 112–120.

Wilson, K. B., Karg, A., & Ghaderi, H. (2022). Prospecting non-fungible tokens in the digital economy: Stakeholders and ecosystem, risk and opportunity. *Business Horizons*, 65(5), 657–670.

Wong, S., Yeung, J. K. W., Lau, Y. Y., & Kawasaki, T. (2023). A case study of how maersk adopts cloud-based blockchain integrated with machine learning for sustainable practices. *Sustainability*, 15(9), 7305.

World Tourism Organization. (2020). International Tourism Highlights. Report Edition 2020. www.e-unwto.org/doi/pdf/10.18111/9789284422456

World Travel & Tourism Council. 2019. Economic Impact Research. Available online https://wttc.org/research/economic-impact

Xiang, F., Huaimin, W., Peichang, S., Xue, O., & Xunhui, Z. (2021). Jointgraph: A DAG-based efficient consensus algorithm for consortium blockchains. *Software: Practice and Experience*, 51(10), 1987–1999.

Xu, C., & Sun, Y. (2024). Deciphering trust mechanisms in blockchain platforms: A multifaceted experimental exploration. *Managerial and Decision Economics*, 45(5), 2686–2699.

References   169

Yaga, D., Mell, P., Roby, N., & Scarfone, K. (2019). Blockchain technology overview (No. NIST Internal or Interagency Report (NISTIR) 8202 (Draft)). National Institute of Standards and Technology. https://doi.org/10.6028/NIST.IR.8202.

Yang, C. S. (2019). Maritime shipping digitalization: Blockchain-based technology applications, future improvements, and intention to use. *Transportation Research Part E: Logistics and Transportation Review*, *131*, 108–117.

Ying, W., Jia, S., & Du, W. (2018). Digital enablement of blockchain: Evidence from HNA group. *International Journal of Information Management*, *39*, 1–4.

Zhang, R., Xue, R., & Liu, L. (2019). Security and privacy on blockchain. *ACM Computing Surveys (CSUR)*, *52*(3), 1–34.

Zhang, Y., Wang, Q., Chen, S., & Wang, C. (2023). How to rationally select your delegatee in pos. https://doi.org/10.48550/arXiv.2310.08895.

Zheng, Z., Xie, S., Dai, H., Chen, X., & Wang, H. (2017, June). An overview of blockchain technology: Architecture, consensus, and future trends. In *2017 IEEE International Congress on Big Data (BigData Congress)* (pp. 557–564). IEEE.

Zwitter, A. (2014). Big data ethics. *Big Data & Society*, *1*(2), 1–6.

Zwitter, A., & Hazenberg, J. (2020). Decentralized network governance: Blockchain technology and the future of regulation. *Frontiers in Blockchain*, *3*, 12.

Index

adoption of blockchain: appropriate blockchain type selection 102; awareness of blockchain's benefits 77, 110–111, 133, 138; blockchain-as-a-service providers 144; collaborative approach 138; customer receptivity 129; education and training 114, 135, 143; enhancing user experience crucial to 134–135; energy efficiency challenges 76, 77, 78–79, 101, 104, 109, 110, 124; engaging local communities 79–80; exclusion challenges 121; financial incentive schemes and technical support 77–78, 79; gamification strategies 138–139; government engagement, need for 119; high failure rate of blockchain startups 139; high investment costs 77, 100, 102, 108, 110, 143–144; high operational costs 108, 109; high-profile failures 140–142; high transaction fees on some networks 21, 77; infrastructure deficit 102; inherent delays in transaction authorization processes 102–103; large corporations leading uptake 111; legacy systems, integration with 139; managerial openness to 133–134; market uncertainty 104; network latency 103; platform selection 138; project goals,

need for clarity about 142–143, 144; public and private sector collaboration for supportive ecosystem 135; reluctance of businesses to embrace disruptive technology 105; scalability challenges 76, 101–102, 109, 138, 139; skilled worker shortage 100, 102, 104; stakeholder buy-in 143; standardization and interoperability challenges 22, 76–77, 79, 101, 103, 104, 115, 125; standards and certifications, need for 113–114; trust barrier 120; user-friendliness challenges 120–121, 134–135; *see also* regulation and compliance
agriculture 53
agrotourism 127, 132
Airbnb 35, 48, 136
Alastria project 48
Aloha community engagement platform 81–82
artificial intelligence (AI) 34, 35, 37, 45, 48, 123, 134, 135
Aruba 129
augmented reality 35, 37, 47
Australian Securities Exchange 141
AXA 93

baggage tracking 94–95, 130
bAirbnb 136–137
banking industry 53
BedSwap 95

Index 171

Beenest App 49
Bext360 sustainable supply chain
   management 81
Bhutan 46
Bitcoin 8, 19, 32, 44, 55, 76, 84, 85,
   88, 103, 104, 108, 110, 125, 133,
   137
BitConnect 140
blockchain: basic process of
   6, 10–11, 28–29, 32–33, 42;
   collaboration and efficiency
   fostered by 31; consortium
   blockchains 125; decentralization
   as essential feature 5, 6, 10,
   11, 13, 15, 27–28, 42, 65; as
   distributed ledger 6–7, 10–11, 15;
   immutability, as core principle
   11–12, 16; innovation fostered
   by 28, 53, 146; main applications
   of 51–53, 84; public vs. private
   55, 102, 125; trust, security, and
   transparency 2, 5–6, 6–7, 10,
   11, 12, 27, 29–31, 35, 42–43,
   73, 74, 120, 130, 147; versatile
   technology, evolution into 10
Booking.com 48
booking systems: airline
   overbooking burdens,
   alleviation of 87; automation 86;
   intermediaries, elimination of
   7–8, 12, 13, 17–18, 43–44, 86,
   95; real-time information 129;
   security, transparency, and trust
   8, 12, 17, 18, 43, 86; speculation,
   prevention of 87; streamlining for
   efficiency 87, 95; unauthorized
   sales, prevention of 87; see also
   smart contracts
bottlenecks in blockchain processing
   21

California Consumer Privacy Act
   107–108
Canada 1
Cardano 102
cargo tracking 94
Caribbean 49, 85
China 1, 84, 106, 129

Cloud computing 53, 124
Coincheck 137
consensus mechanisms: crucial role of
   7; delegated PoS (DPoS) 7; hacker
   vulnerability 106; proof-based vs.
   vote-based 55–56; proof of stake
   (PoS) 5–6, 7, 77, 102; proof of
   work (PoW) 5–6, 7, 29, 102, 124
COVID-19 pandemic 10, 39, 67, 87
Croatia 137
crowdfunding 52, 75
cryptocurrencies: consumer
   confidence in 84–85; energy-
   efficient algorithms 124;
   global acceptance of 19, 44,
   85; government restrictions on
   105–106; hacker vulnerability
   103; initial coin offerings 130;
   intermediaries, elimination of
   44; low transaction fees 19,
   85; loyalty programs 85, 88;
   as most prominent application
   of blockchain 52; multi-chains
   accommodating different
   currencies 108–109; public
   awareness and understanding,
   lack of 133; regulatory and legal
   uncertainties 76, 106; scalability
   issues, potential remedies to 102;
   small economies benefited by
   132; as transformative force 83;
   user-friendly interfaces 134–135;
   see also Bitcoin; Ethereum
cryptography: cryptographic hashing
   5, 6, 11, 32, 122; homomorphic
   encryption 118; as key pillar of
   blockchain 15; public and private
   keys 15, 32; robustness of, as
   ethical concern 124; secure multi-
   party computation 118
CryptoKitties 102
cybersecurity 53, 103, 106,
   121–122, 139, 140

decentralized applications (DApps)
   27, 102
Decentralized Autonomous
   Organization (DAO) 140

172 *Index*

decentralized travel ecosystems 25
Deutsche Börse 141
DidaTravel 129
Digital Catapult 48
digital divide 24
digital nomads 36, 37
Dubai 48, 90, 95

Eclipse attack 103
e-commerce platforms 85–86
EOS 102
Ethereum 8, 19, 33, 44, 49, 52, 55,
  62, 76, 103, 110, 133, 140
Etherisc App 49
ethical considerations with
  blockchain: agrotourism,
  promotion of 127; challenging
  centralized data monopolies
  136–137; corruption, blockchain
  as tool against 126–127, 132;
  democratizing access to travel
  services 127; democratizing of
  data control 27–28, 31; disruptive
  force, blockchain as 124; donation
  platforms 137; empowerment
  of small- and medium-sized
  enterprises 127; environmental
  impacts 124; longevity of
  platforms 123–124; neutrality
  of blockchain ecosystem 124,
  127, 132, 147; respect for human
  dignity, in interactions with
  technology 123; robustness of
  cryptography 124; sustainable and
  diverse blockchain communities
  125; *see also* regulation and
  compliance; sustainability
European Union (EU) 59, 123, 147;
  see also General Data Protection
  Regulation
experiential travel 36, 37

Financial Action Task Force 126
Food Chain 96
FTX project 143

General Data Protection Regulation
  (EU) 59, 105, 107, 117–118, 122,
  126, 143, 148

Germany 141
globalization, potential of
  blockchain to improve 147
GoEureka (GOT) 49
Google 35
Green Key 35
Grin crypto donation platform 81
Guaranteed Entrance Token protocol
  87
guest tracking for hotels 95

healthcare 53
health and safety information
  management 39–40, 53, 67, 72,
  130, 132
Hyperledger 138

IBM 138, 139, 142
Iceland 45–46
identity management: biometric
  identification 46, 91, 93,
  130–131; identity theft,
  prevention of 91–92, 93,
  131; integrating digital IDs
  with reservations 91; privacy
  protections 18–19, 43, 91, 93;
  security 8, 18, 91; self-sovereign
  identity 15, 18–19, 43, 68, 132;
  streamlining for efficiency 8, 18,
  19, 91, 92–94, 131; universal
  traveler identity 91, 93
Impact Travel Alliance sustainable
  tourism education 82
insurance industry 53
International Air Transport
  Association 126
International Chamber of Commerce
  60
International Organization for
  Standardization 60
Internet of Things (IoT) 25–26, 34,
  45, 53, 96, 137, 146
Italy 61, 96

Japan 1, 137
Jumeirah Group 90

Korea 84, 122
KrisPay 85, 88

Index 173

Latin America 85
LEED 35
Litecoin 55, 110
LockTrip 48
Long Blockchain Corp 141
loyalty programs: aggregation of
information 88; interoperability
across service providers 9, 20,
44, 75, 89, 128, 130; managing
unredeemed reward liabilities
88; secure and transparent
transactions 9, 20, 44, 66, 87,
131; smart contracts 54, 57, 61;
streamlining for efficiency 89;
tokenized loyalty points 20, 88,
89–90
Loyyal 90

Marriott 93
MetaMask 134–135
microfinancing 75
Moldova 127
Moller-Maersk 139, 142
Monero 110

Netherlands 87
Nimiq 134
Nordic Choice Hotels 86

Open Zeppelin 64

P2P marketplaces 13, 26
Parity Multisig Wallet 141
payment processing: currency
exchange 19–20, 44; fees
reduction 8, 12, 19, 44, 71, 74,
86; intermediaries, elimination of
8, 12, 16, 19, 21, 44, 67, 71, 74,
84, 86; processing time reduction
8, 12, 19, 21, 44, 71, 74, 84,
86; security and transparency
8, 15, 21, 44, 71, 86; simplified
cross-border transactions 16,
19–20; smart contracts 54, 57;
see also e-commerce platforms;
tokenization of assets and
services
pricing and fees: hidden fees and
opaque pricing, traditional

problem of 14; transparency and
consistency 14
privacy: controlled data sharing
122; as cornerstone of blockchain
technology 122; data protection
standards, need for 123;
inaccuracies in personal data 122;
potential conflicts of blockchain
with data privacy regulations 22,
59, 76, 78, 79, 101, 105, 107,
116, 122, 126; raw data security
122; right to be forgotten 118,
122, 126, 148; transparency of
pertinent information 122–123;
see also General Data Protection
Regulation
Prodeum 140–141
public–private partnerships 42

regulation and compliance:
accountability 16; anti-money
laundering regulations 22, 105,
106, 107, 125–126; auditing
process 16, 123; case-by-case
assessment of competition
issues 118–119; complexity of
navigating 10, 12; consumer
protection as paramount 125;
counter-terrorism financing
regulations 105, 106; cross-
jurisdictional harmonization,
need for 114–115, 126; data
privacy regulations, difficulty of
reconciling with transparency
22, 59, 76, 78, 79, 101, 105,
107, 116, 122, 148; enforcement
mechanisms, need for 117;
frameworks for regulator
cooperation, need for 114–115;
government restrictions on
cryptocurrencies 105–106;
guidance on compliance, need
for 118; intellectual property
regulations, potential blockchain
conflicts with 22; know-your-
customer regulations 107,
125–126; law enforcement
training, need for 116; legal
recognition of blockchain

174 *Index*

elements, need for 113; liability frameworks, need for 117; privacy-enhancing technologies, need for 118; regulatory clarity, need for 115, 123; regulatory sandboxes 60, 116; roles and responsibilities, defining for accountability purposes 116–117; uncertain and evolving state of regulatory landscape 22, 58–60, 63, 76, 101, 104, 105–108, 109–110, 115, 125; *see also* General Data Protection Regulation

reviews and ratings: fake reviews problem 14, 69, 97–98, 132; transparency and authenticity of blockchain-based reviews 14, 60, 97–98, 127–128, 132

Rijeka Marketplace 137

Romania 129

SAP Blockchain 138

Singapore 60, 85, 87, 88

SITA 93, 94

Slock.it 97

small economies, benefits of blockchain for 132–133

smart contracts: authority of, vs. human agents 123; automation as central tenet of 56, 138; booking processes 8, 17, 43, 54, 57, 58, 66, 126; code auditing 63; code vulnerabilities 58, 62–63; coding practices 64; conditional payments 18; data privacy concerns 59, 63; digital keys 97; dispute reduction 18; efficiency gains 53–54, 56, 57, 58, 61, 96; food service industry 97; at heart of blockchain technology 51; hacker vulnerability 106; human error minimized 54, 56, 61; innovation and collaboration fostered by 57–58; insurance policies 53, 97, 129; intermediaries, elimination of 53, 56, 57, 66; interoperability 60, 61;

legal and regulatory framework, uncertain and evolving 22, 58–60, 63; legal and technical complexity of 59; limited legal remedies 59; loyalty programs 54, 57, 61; payment processes 54, 57, 126; pioneered by Ethereum 52, 62; proactive engagement with regulators 64; regulatory compliance, streamlining of 12, 138; regulatory sandboxes for 60; revenue recognition in airline industry 97; security, transparency, and trustworthiness 54, 55, 56, 57, 62; self-regulatory frameworks 60; tax compliance 85; Turkish–Italian hotel operator strategic partnership 61

Smart Trip platform 48

Spain 48

supply chain management: in agriculture 53; counterfeiting prevention 53; immutability and transparency 11–12, 20–21; inventory management 95; real-time visibility of complex supply chains 9, 21; streamlining of logistics processes 9, 21, 132; sustainable food management 67–68, 74–75, 95–96

sustainability: in Bhutan's tourism 46; challenges of integrating blockchain for sustainability 72–73, 76; collaboration between stakeholders 41–42; comprehensive tourism management plans 41; degradation of local cultures 65; economic sustainability 70–71; education and awareness 41, 68, 70; eliminating intermediaries, local economies boosted by 67, 74; environmental pollution 65; fair trade 72; financial tools for local communities 75; food supply, sustainable management of 68, 74–75; global collaboration networks 69–70, 73; high energy

Index 175

demands of blockchain 76, 77, 78–79, 101, 104, 109, 110, 124; in Iceland's tourism 45–46; local community engagement 71–72; localized digital currencies 67; as major challenge in tourism 38, 65; over-consumption of natural resources 65; over-tourism 40–41; public transport 41; renewable energy 41; reliable reviews and ratings for sustainable businesses 69, 74, 75; responsible tourism 74; reward systems for sustainable behavior 68–69, 75–76; smart cities 69, 73; strategic approach to blockchain integration 80; sustainability monitoring 67, 73, 128, 132, 148; Sustainable Development Goals 65, 70; sustainable tourism, definition of 66; sustainable tourism policies 69; tourist satisfaction 68; transparent records of environmental impact 45; as trend in tourism 35, 37, 41, 65; *see also* Aloha community engagement platform; Bext360 sustainable supply chain management; Grin crypto donation platform; Impact Travel Alliance sustainable tourism education; Winding Tree reservation system

Swiss Digital Exchange 141
Switzerland 60, 85, 95
Sybil attack 103

tax compliance 85
Terra project 143
terrorism and political instability 38–39
Thomas Cook 129
tokenization of assets and services 26, 71, 75–76, 85
Tourism 2.0 48, 95
tourism, travel, and hospitality: challenges and opportunities 9; data security and privacy challenges 10, 12, 14; digital transformation 1, 5, 34, 37, 46–47; as driver of global economy 34, 49–50; dynamic nature 2; fragmentation, inefficiency of 10; global turnover and employment 10, 34; intermediaries, inefficiency of 10; multiple and diverse stakeholders 5, 9; research on blockchain adoption 23–25; security challenges 38; transformational potential of blockchain 2, 6, 9, 13, 16, 23–24, 26, 35, 42, 45, 83, 98, 131, 136, 146–147; transparency, historical lack of 10, 42; trust as foundational to 39–40, 43; as vast and complex ecosystem 9–10, 49
tourism information management 66
TradeLens 139, 142
transaction cost economics 147
TravelChain 48
travel technologies market 1
Trippki 90
TUI Group 47, 93, 95, 96, 97, 98
Turkey 61

Uber 137
United Kingdom 48, 60
United States 1, 38, 85, 107

virtual reality 35, 37, 47, 135
voting systems 52

Webjet 47–48
We Trade 143
WICKET 87
Winding Tree reservation system 47, 80–81, 85–86, 95
World Travel and Tourism Council 126

zero-knowledge proofs 78, 93, 116, 118